Campbell's
100 BEST RECIPES
Plus 157 Other Family Favorites and Party Dishes

Recipes developed and tested by Home Economists of Campbell Kitchens
Campbell Soup Company, Camden, N.J.
Fourth Printing — August, 1977

Photographer • Al Gommi
Artist • Joan Blume
Art Director • Gerard Nook
Contributing Editor • Kay Shaw Nelson

CONTENTS

INTRODUCTION

Good food is one of those universal pleasures that transcends time, place, and particulars. Everyone, everywhere has the capacity to appreciate it, whether it arrives at the table as classic Beef Bourguignonne or as a simple potato baked to fluffy perfection. Truly great dishes, both peasant and patrician, satisfy the spirit as well as the appetite, and it is in this tradition that we present "Campbell's 100 Best Recipes."

Over the years Campbell's has provided American families with thousands of imaginative recipes using condensed soups, all thoroughly tested for taste and workability by our test kitchen home economists. In commemoration of the Company's 100th Anniversary in 1969, it seemed appropriate to select the top 100 recipes from our extensive files — no easy task, considering the great number of favorites. After much sifting, reviewing, and reminiscing, we made the selections for this unique volume, and included, (for good measure), another 157 equally appealing recipes.

The result is a book especially suited to all lovers of good food who lack the time usually associated with its preparation. These days, that probably includes just about everyone.

Because of the availability of high-quality, versatile convenience foods like condensed soups, it is no longer necessary to spend hours in food preparation to create delicious dishes. "Cooking with Campbell's", long a way of life in many homes, is an especially appropriate byword today.

Now sauces such as Hollandaise are almost as easy as opening a can of Cream of Celery Soup. Classics like Crab Louis and Chicken Tetrazzini are ready in minutes, minus the fussing. And that traditional menu stand-by, hamburger, takes on new flavor vitality in dishes like Meatballs Oriental and Meatza Pizza.

If you agree with the words of an early American fireplace motto, "The glory of the house is hospitality," then you will certainly relish the many exciting ideas for entertaining that follow. They include menus and recipes for everything from a bring-the-children brunch to a fondue funfest; from an Italian Trattoria buffet to a regal luncheon.

You'll also discover a glorious abundance of internationally inspired dishes as well as an entire chapter devoted to that great American institution, barbecuing. There are robust casseroles for hefty appetites and slenderizing suggestions for calorie-conscious cooks. Teens will enjoy Souperburgers, while tots will love our Souper-Snacks. You'll be serving seconds from the vegetable plate when you make Baked Stuffed Tomatoes and Honey Glazed Sweet Potatoes.

But enough. Turn the page and experience for yourself the rich diversity of the world's eating heritage coupled with contemporary convenience. We hope this collection of Campbell's recipes will assist you in enjoying them both to the fullest.

The "100 Best Recipes" are marked with this symbol . . . ✻

APPETIZERS

A prime virtue of the appetizer is that its culinary role is well defined and easy to comprehend. These tasty tidbits, whether a few or a selection, are designed to enchant the eye, please the palate, and whet the appetite. The marvelous morsels may be canapes, spreads, dips, relishes or more elaborate hot combinations. Make them as pretty as possible, for as openers to any gastronomic get-together they set the scene; even if their appearance is brief, it is, nevertheless, extremely important.

Like so many of our culinary customs, the enjoyment of appetizers is anything but new. Ancient Greeks relished a few "provocatives to drinking," as they were then dubbed, with goblets of wine. The *gustatio*, or first course, of the Romans was an elaborate array of dishes of many kinds and tastes. In Europe it has long been customary to begin any repast with a glittering, taste-tempting appetizer assortment. In Russia there is the galaxy of *zakuski*. Scandinavia has its bountiful *smorgasbord*. Italians are devotees of *antipasto*, and in France there are the heavenly hors d'oeuvres. Austrians and Germans adore their varied and inviting *vorseeisen*. In sunny Spain the pre-meal snacks, *tapas*, include an amazing selection of seafood.

Americans have borrowed from these cuisines and many of the European dishes are now part of our appetizer repertoire. In general, however, we favor easy-to-prepare finger foods, or perhaps a small portion of a flavorful dish. Appetizers are a definite part of our entertainment schedule. They may be served with beverages before a meal, or in lieu of a first course at the table.

Snappy Clam Dip

1 can (10¾ ounces) condensed
    cream of celery soup
1 package (8 ounces) cream
    cheese, softened

1 can (7½ ounces) minced clams,
    well-drained
1 tablespoon chopped parsley
2 teaspoons prepared horseradish

With rotary beater or slow speed of mixer, blend soup into cream cheese. Beat just until blended. Mix in clams, parsley, and horseradish. Chill. Serve with crackers or chips. Makes 2½ cups dip.

Eggs a la Russe

1 can (10¾ ounces) condensed
    cream of celery soup
¼ cup mayonnaise
¼ cup chili sauce
1 tablespoon chopped stuffed
    olives

1 tablespoon finely chopped onion
1 tablespoon chopped parsley
1 teaspoon dried chives
1 teaspoon lemon juice
Dash hot pepper sauce
6 hard-cooked eggs, halved

Combine all ingredients except eggs. Chill. For each serving, arrange 2 egg halves flat side down on dish; top with about ¼ cup sauce. 6 servings.

❋ Cocktail Meatballs or Frankfurters

So simple and so good, these meatballs can be shaped and refrigerated hours before the party. Then it's a breeze to brown and heat them in sauce shortly before serving.

1 pound ground beef
1 egg, slightly beaten
2 tablespoons fine dry bread crumbs
½ teaspoon salt
½ cup finely chopped onion
⅓ cup finely chopped green pepper
2 tablespoons butter or margarine

1 can (10¾ ounces)
    condensed tomato soup
2 tablespoons brown sugar
1 tablespoon vinegar
1 tablespoon Worcestershire
1 teaspoon prepared mustard
Dash hot pepper sauce

Mix *thoroughly* beef, egg, bread crumbs, and salt; shape into 50 small meatballs (½ inch). Arrange in shallow baking pan (12x8x2 inches). Broil 4 inches from heat until browned; turn once. Pour off fat. Meanwhile, in saucepan, cook onion and green pepper in butter until tender. Add meatballs and remaining ingredients. Cover; cook over low heat 10 minutes. Stir occasionally. Makes about 3½ cups.

Cocktail Frankfurters: Substitute 1½ pounds frankfurters, cut in 1-inch pieces for meatball mixture. Proceed as above.

Crab on Toast

1/4 cup finely chopped green onion
1/4 cup finely chopped green
   pepper
2 small cloves garlic, minced
2 tablespoons butter or margarine
1 can (10¾ ounces) condensed
   cream of mushroom soup
1½ cups flaked cooked crab meat

2 tablespoons finely chopped ripe
   olives
1 teaspoon lemon juice
Generous dash hot pepper sauce
20 slices toast, cut in half
   diagonally*
¾ cup shredded Cheddar, Swiss,
   or grated Parmesan cheese

In saucepan, cook onion, green pepper, and garlic in butter until tender. Stir in remaining ingredients except toast and cheese. Place 1 tablespoon crab mixture on each piece of toast. Top each with cheese. Broil 4 inches from heat until cheese melts. Makes 40 appetizers.

*Or use 40 slices melba toast or whole rye crackers.

Liver Pate

Pate:

2 packages (8 ounces each)
   frozen chicken livers
1 can (10¾ ounces) condensed
   cream of mushroom soup
1 cup chopped onion

2 eggs
1/4 cup milk
1/8 teaspoon pepper
1/8 teaspoon thyme, crushed
1/4 cup fine dry bread crumbs

In saucepan, cook frozen livers in boiling water 15 minutes or until done; drain. In blender at high speed, beat soup, onion, eggs, milk, pepper, and thyme until smooth. At low speed, gradually add livers and bread crumbs. Pour into loaf pan (8x4x3 inches); place in shallow pan with 1-inch deep water. Bake at 325°F. for 1½ hours or until silver knife inserted in center comes out clean. *Refrigerate overnight.*

Glaze:

2 tablespoons butter or margarine
2 tablespoons flour
1/2 cup condensed chicken broth
2 teaspoons unflavored gelatin

1/4 cup water
2 tablespoons heavy cream
Generous dash white pepper
Parsley

In saucepan, melt butter; blend in flour. Gradually add broth. Cook, stirring until thickened and smooth. In small saucepan, sprinkle gelatine over water; stir over low heat until gelatine is dissolved. Blend into sauce with cream and pepper. *Cool to room temperature.*

Unmold pate. Pour glaze evenly over top and sides. (Glaze should set on contact with *chilled* pate.) Garnish with parsley. 10 to 12 servings.

Pâté, meaning in French "pie," may be served hot or cold. Achieve variety by cooking in molds of different shapes and by using pretty garnishes like vegetable strips, flowers, slices, rings or dices. Serve attractively.

❋ Cheese Fondue

Recipe may be doubled

1 cup Sauterne or other dry
   white wine
1 large clove garlic, minced
1 pound natural Swiss cheese,
   cubed or shredded

1/4 cup flour
1 can (11 ounces) condensed
   Cheddar cheese soup
French or Italian bread cubes*

In saucepan or fondue pot, simmer wine and garlic. Combine cheese and flour; gradually blend into wine. Heat until cheese melts; stir often. Blend in soup. Heat, stirring until smooth. Spear bread with fork or toothpick and dip into fondue. Makes about 4 cups.
*Also use bite-size pieces of cooked artichoke hearts, franks, lobster, or shrimp.

Appetizer Veal Roll-ups

1 1/2 pounds thinly sliced
   veal cutlet
24 canned whole small mushroom
   caps (about 4 1/2 ounces)
1/4 cup chopped onion
1 tablespoon chopped parsley

2 tablespoons butter or margarine
1 can (10 3/4 ounces) condensed
   cream of chicken soup
1/4 cup water
2 tablespoons Madeira wine

Pound veal; cut into 24 pieces (about 2 1/2 inches square). Wrap 1 mushroom cap in each piece veal; fasten with toothpicks or skewers. In skillet, brown roll-ups and cook onion with parsley in butter until tender. Stir in remaining ingredients. Cover; cook over low heat 30 minutes or until veal is tender. Makes 24 small roll-ups.

Blue Cheese Dip

1 package (8 ounces) cream
   cheese, softened
1 can (10 3/4 ounces) condensed
   cream of celery soup

1/2 cup crumbled blue cheese
1/4 cup diced cucumber

Beat cream cheese until smooth; blend in soup. Stir in blue cheese and cucumber. Chill. Serve with crackers or chips. Makes 2 1/2 cups dip.

Serve dips in pretty bowls or in a handsome curly-leafed Savoy cabbage (hollowed out). Vary the dunkers, using creative crackers, toast triangles, vegetable sticks or as in the Middle East, "scoops" of lettuce or cabbage.

Invite guests to a sip and dip party starring this
Cheese Fondue in a pretty earthenware pot or heavy chafing dish.
Offer it with a light dry white wine before a crackling fire.

SOUPS

Close to the hearts of all of us is the marvelous repertoire of savory soups, which can be enjoyed hot or cold on any occasion, and at anytime of day. Broth, consomme, puree, bisque, potage, bouillon or chowder, clear, creamed or thick, soup is a never-fail gastronomic winner. Reliable as an old and trusted friend, it also has the appeal and sparkle of a new acquaintance.

The saga of soup is as old as man himself. For it was pre-historic man who began the art of making soup by dropping some bones, meat, water and heated stones into an animal-skin bag. By the Stone Age soups were simmered in kettles or pots over fires. Thus *Pot au Feu* (Pot on the Fire) was created. The first soup mentioned in writing was made with lentils, the "mess of pottage" for which Esau sold his birthright to Jacob.

For a very long time soup was called potage, broth, brewis or gruel. Its present name was taken from "soppers," which were the bread pieces dipped into meat broth. To soups we are indebted for the name of "restaurant." For in 1765 a Parisian tavern proprietor, one Boulanger, started selling nourishing soups, which he called *restorantes*, restorative snacks or pick-ups.

Over the years the world-wide appeal of soups has transcended geographic and social boundaries. Every country has one or more national favorites. Soup may be basic and robust or complex and subtle. In the old days the stockpot always simmered on the back of the stove, and America is justly proud of the regional specialties its cooks created, as well as many favorites from foreign lands.

Today, you have a dazzling variety of canned condensed soups immediately available. Delectable in themselves, you can quickly and imaginatively make your own new soup creations by combining two or more of them. There are many popular soup-mates and the combinations are endless. Such is the versatility of soup that a nuance of flavor or a bit of color may give an old favorite fresh appeal and attraction. You may work wonders with a touch of spice, a dash of sherry, a sprinkling of herbs, grated cheese, toasted nuts of croutons, or a dollop of sour or whipped cream.

Let it be steaming hot or frosty cold. Serving soup is fun. Spoon it from a large bowl, pour it from a pitcher, or ladle it from a tureen.

Soup is a standby for all social occasions. As a prelude to a meal, a delicate first course or a main dish. Its warming goodness is delicious with salads or sandwiches. As a snack it is perfect from midmorning to midnight. Soup is the answer to coping with unexpected guests, and is excellent for entertaining large numbers.

TAKE YOUR CHOICE

Are the children hungry but uninterested? Chicken & stars, tomato-beef noodle-O's, chicken noodle-O's and chicken 'n dumplings will intrigue and nourish. So will "Souper-snacks" made with cream of chicken, green pea or vegetable.

Is the male animal roaring for his food? Call on the "Manhandlers," such as bean with bacon, beef, chili beef, minestrone, noodles & ground beef, split pea with ham, clam chowder (Manhattan style or New England), oyster stew, Scotch broth or vegetable beef.

Does the menu for a special dinner party need a first course? Sophisticated golden mushroom, black bean, cream of mushroom or consomme will set the pace with distinction.

Are the bathroom scales out of order? Possibly. But try the "Slim Six" before buying new scales. Beef broth, chicken broth, chicken gumbo, consomme, onion and old fashioned vegetable . . . each is under 60 calories per seven-ounce cup.

Is the household budget out of balance? Soup can't solve the problem but it has always helped.

To broaden your acquaintance with appealing soups, here are serving ideas and specialties from our collection.

Souper Snacks

Need a wee morsel to sustain you through the next 2 hours before dinner or to welcome the children home from school? And what do you serve when the bridge players stay late but vote down the standard rich dessert with coffee routine? Reach to the soup shelf for a snack that's warming and always pleasingly good.

Is your preference for "Soup and Crackers" . . . or are you in favor of "Soup and Crunch," such as piping hot tomato alongside golden carrot sticks? With mixing and matching, you're bound to come up with just the right tidbit to suit snackers.

Chicken 'n Dumplings . . . . *Apple slices sandwiched with peanut butter*
Green Pea . . . . *Round butter crackers or saltines*
Chicken Noodle . . . . *Popcorn or peanuts*
Vegetable . . . . *Bologna rolled around pickle strip*
Chili Beef . . . . *Green pepper rings or corn chips*
Onion . . . . *Celery filled with cottage cheese or shredded wheat crackers*
Cream of Potato . . . . *Fresh orange wedges*
Golden Vegetable Noodle-O's . . . . *Cheese cubes*

Chinese Noodle Soup

1 cup sliced mushrooms (about ¼ pound)	2 soup cans water
2 tablespoons butter or margarine	1½ cups cooked shrimp
2 cans (10¾ ounces each) condensed beef noodle soup	2 tablespoons chopped watercress
	4 teaspoons soy sauce

In saucepan, brown mushrooms in butter. Add remaining ingredients. Heat; stir occasionally. Makes about 6 cups.

Pennsylvania Dutch Chowder

½ cup sliced celery	1½ soup cans water
½ cup chopped onion	1 can (8 ounces) whole kernel corn
2 tablespoons butter or margarine	Generous dash pepper
2 cans (10½ ounces each) condensed chicken 'n dumplings soup	

In saucepan, cook celery and onion in butter until tender. Add remaining ingredients. Heat; stir occasionally. Makes about 5½ cups.

This hearty dish probably originated in New England but today each American locale has a specialty. The name derives from France where a chaudière is a short-legged kettle.

Pasta Fagioli

2 tablespoons chopped parsley
¼ teaspoon rosemary, crushed
1 medium clove garlic, minced
2 tablespoons olive oil
1 can (11½ ounces) condensed
   bean with bacon soup

1 soup can water
1 teaspoon tomato paste
Generous dash pepper
½ cup cooked elbow macaroni

In saucepan, cook parsley, rosemary, and garlic in oil until parsley is wilted. Stir in soup, water, tomato paste, and pepper; add macaroni. Heat; stir occasionally. Makes about 2½ cups.

Potage Senegalese

1 can (10¾ ounces) condensed
   cream of chicken soup
1 soup can water
½ cup light cream
¼ cup applesauce

2 tablespoons shredded coconut
1 teaspoon curry powder
½ teaspoon garlic salt
½ teaspoon onion powder
1 avocado, sliced

In saucepan, combine all ingredients except avocado. Heat; stir occasionally. Top each serving with avocado. Makes about 3½ cups.
For chilled soup: Prepare recipe as above; chill 6 hours. Serve in chilled bowls.

Black Bean Double Hot

⅓ cup chopped onion
2 tablespoons butter or margarine
1 can (11 ounces) condensed
   black bean soup
1 soup can water

2 teaspoons chopped hot cherry
   peppers
1 teaspoon lemon or lime juice
¼ cup coarsely crushed tortilla
   chips
Lime slices

In saucepan, cook onion in butter until tender. Stir in soup; gradually blend in water. Add peppers and lemon or lime juice. Heat: stir occasionally. Just before serving stir in tortilla chips. Garnish with lime slices. Makes about 2½ cups.

Consomme Parfait

1 can (10½ ounces) condensed
   consomme

¼ cup yogurt
2 tablespoons chopped parsley

Place unopened can of consomme in refrigerator until jellied, at least 4 hours. To serve, spoon consomme in small sherbet glasses; top with yogurt and chopped parsley. Makes about 1 cup.

Vegetable Salami Chowder

½ cup salami strips
2 tablespoons butter or margarine
1 can (10½ ounces) condensed
  old fashioned vegetable soup

1 soup can water
½ cup chopped canned tomatoes
1 teaspoon prepared horseradish
Garlic flavored croutons

In saucepan, brown salami in butter. Add soup, water, tomatoes, and horseradish. Heat; stir occasionally. Garnish with croutons. Makes about 3 cups.

French Onion Soup

1 can (10½ ounces) condensed
  onion soup
1 soup can water

3 thin slices French bread, toasted
¾ cup grated Gruyere or Swiss
  cheese

In saucepan, combine soup and water; heat. In individual serving bowls, place a slice of French bread; top with cheese. Pour in hot soup. Makes about 2½ cups.
Broiler Method: Pour heated soup into individual oven-proof serving bowls. Place bread on top; sprinkle with cheese. Broil until cheese melts.

This soup's main ingredient was once a "weather predictor" according to an old rhyme. "Onion's skin is very thin, Mild weather's coming in, Onion's skin is thick and tough, Coming winter's cold and rough."

Marriage Soup Italiano

1 can (10¾ ounces) condensed
  cream of chicken soup
1 cup light cream

1 can (10¾ ounces) condensed
  chicken noodle soup
½ cup milk
2 tablespoons grated Parmesan
  cheese

In saucepan, blend cream of chicken soup and cream; add remaining ingredients. Heat; stir occasionally. Makes about 4 cups.

Tropical Fruit Soup

1 can (10¾ ounces) condensed
  cream of chicken soup
1 soup can milk
1 teaspoon lime juice

½ cup mashed ripe banana
½ cup seedless grapes, halved
Grated lime rind
Ground nutmeg

In saucepan, blend soup, milk, and lime juice. Heat; stir occasionally. Chill 6 hours or more. Just before serving, blend in banana; stir in grapes. Garnish with rind and nutmeg. Makes about 3 cups.

*Pages 20-21: America's favorite lunch . . . Soup and Sandwiches.
Soups shown are: Split Pea Potage, Chicken-Vegetable Noodle-O's,
Barbecue Bean and California Bisque.*

❋ Split Pea Potage

¼ cup chopped onion
1 medium clove garlic, minced
2 tablespoons butter or margarine
1 can (11½ ounces) condensed
  split pea with ham soup

1 soup can water
2 tablespoons sherry
½ cup chopped canned tomatoes

In saucepan, cook onion with garlic in butter until tender. Stir in soup; gradually blend in water. Add sherry and tomatoes. Heat; stir occasionally. Makes about 2½ cups.

❋ Vichyssoise

1 can (10¾ ounces) condensed
  cream of potato soup

1 soup can milk or ½ light cream
  and ½ milk
Chopped chives, mint, or parsley

In saucepan, combine soup and milk. Heat; stir occasionally. Beat until smooth with blender; or use rotary beater or electric mixer and strain. Chill 6 hours or more. Thin to desired consistency. Serve in chilled bowls. Garnish with chives, mint, or parsley. Makes about 2½ cups.

❋ Barbecue Bean Soup

½ cup green pepper strips
⅓ cup chopped onion
1 medium clove garlic, minced
2 tablespoons butter or margarine
1 can (11¼ ounces) condensed
  hot dog bean soup

1 soup can water
1 tablespoon chili sauce or
  ketchup
½ teaspoon prepared mustard
⅛ teaspoon hot pepper sauce

In saucepan, cook pepper and onion with garlic in butter until tender. Stir in soup; gradually blend in water. Add remaining ingredients. Heat; stir occasionally. Makes about 3 cups.

California Bisque

¼ cup thinly sliced celery
1 tablespoon butter or margarine
1 can (11 ounces) condensed
  tomato bisque soup

1 soup can water
½ medium avocado, diced
2 teaspoons lemon juice

In saucepan, cook celery in butter until tender. Add remaining ingredients. Heat; stir occasionally. Makes about 3 cups.

"Soup puts the heart at ease, calms down the violence of hunger, eliminates the tensions of the day, and awakens and refines the appetite."
ESCOFFIER.

Oyster Stew Orientale

1/2 cup chopped onion
2 tablespoons butter or margarine
1 can (10 1/2 ounces) condensed
   oyster stew
1 soup can milk

1 tablespoon toasted sesame
   seeds
Cooked rice
Chopped chives

In saucepan, cook onion in butter until tender. Add soup, milk, and sesame seeds. Heat; stir occasionally. Serve about 1/4 cup rice in each bowl. Garnish with chives. Makes about 2 1/2 cups.

Caldo Verde

2 cups spinach leaves cut in thin
   strips
1 tablespoon olive oil

1 can (10 3/4 ounces) condensed
   cream of potato soup
1 soup can water
Generous dash hot pepper sauce

In saucepan, cook spinach in olive oil until tender. Stir in soup, water, and pepper sauce. Heat; stir occasionally. Makes about 2 1/2 cups.

Pot-o-Gold Soup

1 can (10 3/4 ounces) condensed
   chicken broth
3 cups sliced raw carrots (about
   1 pound)
1/4 cup chopped celery

2 tablespoons chopped onion
1 soup can light cream
1/2 soup can milk
1/4 teaspoon nutmeg

In saucepan, combine broth, carrots, celery, and onion. Cover; cook 20 minutes or until carrots are very tender. Blend in electric blender until smooth. In saucepan, combine all ingredients. Heat; stir occasionally. Makes about 4 1/2 cups.
For chilled soup: Chill 6 hours or more. Thin to desired consistency with additional cold milk.

Spanish Garlic Soup

2 medium cloves garlic
2 tablespoons olive oil
2 thin slices French bread

1 can (10 1/2 ounces) condensed
   beef broth
1 soup can water
1 egg, slightly beaten

In saucepan, slowly brown garlic in oil; remove garlic. Add bread; brown. Add broth and water. Cook over low heat 5 minutes; stir to break up bread. Bring to boil; pour egg slowly into soup, stirring constantly. Makes about 2 1/2 cups.

Won Ton Soup

1 egg, slightly beaten
¼ cup water
1 cup flour
¼ teaspoon salt
1 cup finely chopped
* cooked chicken*
1 tablespoon finely chopped
* green onion*

2 tablespoons soy sauce
2 cans (10¾ ounces each)
* condensed chicken broth*
2 soup cans water
½ cup cooked chicken or pork
* cut in strips*
¼ cup chopped spinach

Gradually stir egg and ¼ cup water into flour and salt. Knead on lightly floured board until dough is smooth; roll dough into 15x12-inch piece; cut into 20 squares (3 inch). Thoroughly mix finely chopped chicken, onion, soy, and remaining egg; place a heaping teaspoon of mixture on each square. Bring corners together and seal edges. In saucepan, combine soup and water; bring to boil. Add won tons; cook over low heat 5 minutes. Add chicken strips and spinach. Makes about 7 cups.

Greek Soup

1 can (10½ ounces) condensed
* chicken with rice soup*
1 soup can water

1 egg
1 tablespoon lemon juice
Lemon slices

In saucepan or double boiler, combine soup and water. Cook over *medium heat*. Remove from heat. In a bowl, beat egg until light and frothy; gradually add lemon juice and 1 cup hot broth. Slowly stir egg mixture into soup. Cook a few minutes over *very low heat*, stirring until egg is thoroughly blended with soup. *Do not boil.* Garnish with lemon. Serve immediately. (Overheating will cause curdling.) Makes about 2½ cups.

Stracciatella

1 can (10¾ ounces) condensed
* chicken broth*
1 soup can water
1 egg

2 tablespoons grated Parmesan
* cheese*
1 tablespoon chopped parsley
Dash nutmeg, optional

In saucepan, combine broth and water. Heat. Beat egg with cheese, parsley, and nutmeg; gradually pour into simmering soup, stirring gently until egg is set. Serve immediately. Makes about 2½ cups.

Richly red Tomato Soup warms all occasions. Little folks and oldsters welcome its cheering appearance and irresistible flavor. Serve with finesse and flair from a handsome tureen.

❋ *Zuppa Zingara*

½ pound beef tenderloin or
  sirloin, cut in very thin strips
2 tablespoons salad oil
1 can (10¾ ounces) condensed
  golden mushroom soup
2 cans (10½ ounces each)
  condensed onion soup

1½ soup cans water
¼ cup Burgundy or other dry
  red wine
2 tablespoons chopped parsley
⅛ teaspoon tarragon, crushed

In saucepan, brown beef in oil. Pour off fat. Stir in golden mushroom soup; gradually blend in remaining ingredients. Heat; stir occasionally. Makes about 6 cups.

Vegetable Beef 'n Herb Soup

1 tablespoon finely chopped
  parsley
¼ teaspoon basil, crushed
1 small clove garlic, minced

1 tablespoon butter or margarine
1 can (10½ ounces) condensed
  vegetable beef soup
1 soup can water
Grated Parmesan cheese

In saucepan, cook parsley and basil with garlic in butter until tender. Add soup and water. Heat; stir occasionally. Serve with Parmesan. Makes about 2½ cups.

Soup Mates

Mix two soups to make a new soup. Most everyone enjoys concocting their own variation by mixing and matching different kinds.

Celery Pea Potage

1 can (10¾ ounces) condensed
  cream of celery soup
1 can (11¼ ounces) condensed
  green pea soup

1 soup can milk
1 soup can water

In saucepan, stir soups until smooth; gradually blend in milk and water. Heat; stir occasionally. Makes about 5 cups.

Beef and Vegetable Noodle-O's

1 can (10¾ ounces) condensed
  tomato-beef noodle-O's soup

1 can (10½ ounces) condensed
  vegetable soup
1½ soup cans water

In saucepan, combine all ingredients. Heat; stir occasionally. Makes about 4½ cups.

Offer soup in flowered cups, colorful mugs, or sturdy glasses, deep plates or bowls. For a large party a chafing dish may double as a server-warmer for soup.

All-Star Chicken Soup

1 can (10½ ounces) condensed
  chicken 'n dumplings soup

1 can (10½ ounces) condensed
  chicken & stars soup
1½ soup cans water

In saucepan, combine all ingredients. Heat; stir occasionally. Makes about 4½ cups.

Beef-Eater's Bowl

1 can (10¾ ounces) condensed
  golden mushroom soup

1 can (10¾ ounces) condensed
  noodles & ground beef soup
1½ soup cans water

In saucepan, combine all ingredients. Heat; stir occasionally. Makes about 4½ cups.

Double Chicken Soup

1 can (10¾ ounces) condensed
  cream of chicken soup
1 can (10½ ounces) condensed
  chicken vegetable soup

1 soup can milk
½ soup can water

In saucepan, combine all ingredients. Heat; stir occasionally. Makes about 4½ cups.

Stouthearted Stockpot

1 can (10¾ ounces) condensed
  golden mushroom soup

1 can (11 ounces) condensed
  stockpot soup
1½ soup cans water

In saucepan, combine all ingredients. Heat; stir occasionally. Makes about 4½ cups.

Chicken-Vegetable Noodle-O's

1 can (10½ ounces) condensed
  chicken vegetable soup

1 can (10½ ounces) condensed
  golden vegetable noodle-O's soup
1½ soup cans water

In saucepan, combine all ingredients. Heat; stir occasionally. Makes about 4½ cups.

Creamy Chicken Noodle-O's

1 can (10¾ ounces) condensed
  cream of chicken soup
1 can (10¼ ounces) condensed
  chicken noodle-O's soup

1 soup can milk
½ soup can water

In saucepan, combine all ingredients. Heat; stir occasionally. Makes about 4½ cups.

BEEF

"**W**hen in doubt, serve beef" might well be the motto of the modern host or hostess. Certainly there is no question that beef is the most popular meat in America. Fortunately, it is available in fascinating variety, and you may prepare any number of inviting dishes from a cosmopolitan collection of recipes. Whether braised, roasted, stewed, broiled, baked or barbecued, beef is sure to be a triumph for any social occasion.

Paradoxically, our favorite meat is not native to this hemisphere, since the first cattle came from Europe. Those brought by the Spaniards to the Southwest developed into the world-famous Texas Longhorns and provided not only necessary fare, but colorful folklore as well. The romance of the Western cowboys and their chuck-wagon cookery is a bright page of history and legend.

The various cuts of beef, numbering as many as 45, differ, of course, in quality and flavor. Such superb fare as a standing rib roast or a filet mignon, however, is no more nutritious than a boneless pot roast or a chuck steak.

Two particular beef specialties, steaks and hamburgers, have become national symbols, and their current international popularity is generally associated with America. Steak, however, was a favorite in Merrie Englande, deriving its name from a Saxon term, *on steik*, "a slice of meat roasted on a spit." Ground meats have also been enjoyed through the ages, and our hamburgers were named for the bustling German seaport of Hamburg.

Fortunately, beef has a cosmopolitan appeal, and our gastronomic beef repertoire includes superb dishes from many lands. Modern menu makers have many ways to flavor beef with herbs, spices, wines and sauces. And, these days, convenience foods play a major role in shortening the time it takes to prepare these appealing extra touches.

❋ Beef Burgundy

1 pound sirloin cut into 1-inch
    cubes
2 tablespoons butter or margarine
1 can (10¾ ounces) condensed
    golden mushroom soup
¼ cup Burgundy or other dry
    red wine

12 small whole white onions
    (¾ pound)
2 tablespoons chopped parsley
⅛ teaspoon pepper
Cooked wide noodles

In skillet, brown meat in butter. Add remaining ingredients except noodles. Cover; cook over low heat 1 hour or until tender. Stir occasionally. Serve with noodles. Makes about 3 cups.

In Hungary a variety of flavorful dishes, each seasoned with paprika, are called gulyas, or herdsman's meat. Enriched with sour cream, this is a welcome hearty dish.

❋ Hungarian Goulash

1½ pounds beef cubes (1½ inch)
2 tablespoons shortening
1 can (10¾ ounces) condensed
    tomato soup
½ cup sour cream
¼ cup water

1 cup sliced onion
1 tablespoon paprika
⅛ teaspoon pepper
4 medium potatoes (1½ pounds),
    quartered

In large heavy pan, brown beef in shortening; pour off fat. Stir in remaining ingredients except potatoes. Cover; cook over low heat 1½ hours. Add potatoes. Cook 1 hour more or until meat is tender. Stir occasionally. Makes about 6 cups.

Savory Meatball 'n Spaghetti Bake

1½ pounds ground beef
1 egg, slightly beaten
½ cup fine dry bread crumbs
1 teaspoon salt
1 cup sliced onion
2 cans (10¾ ounces each) condensed
    cream of mushroom soup

1 cup sour cream
1 cup drained chopped
    canned tomatoes
3 cups cooked spaghetti
½ teaspoon dried dill weed, crushed
Grated Parmesan cheese

Mix *thoroughly* beef, egg, bread crumbs, and salt; shape into 24 meatballs. In large heavy pan, brown meatballs and cook onion until tender (use shortening if necessary); pour off fat. Blend in soup, sour cream, tomatoes, spaghetti, and dill. Pour into 3-quart casserole. Bake at 400°F. for 30 minutes or until hot; stir. Sprinkle with cheese. Makes about 9 cups.

Salisbury Steak, Onion Gravy

1 can (10½ ounces) condensed
    onion soup
1½ pounds ground beef
½ cup fine dry bread crumbs
1 egg, slightly beaten
¼ teaspoon salt

Dash pepper
1 tablespoon flour
¼ cup ketchup
¼ cup water
1 teaspoon Worcestershire
½ teaspoon prepared mustard

In bowl, combine ⅓ cup soup with beef, crumbs, egg, salt, and pepper. Shape into 6 oval patties. In skillet, brown patties; pour off fat. Gradually blend remaining soup into flour until smooth. Add to skillet with remaining ingredients; stir to loosen browned bits. Cover; cook over low heat 20 minutes or until done. Stir occasionally. 6 servings.

Barbecue Stew

1½ pounds beef cubes (1½ inch)
2 tablespoons shortening
1 can (10½ ounces) condensed
    beef broth
½ cup water
1 cup sliced onion
¼ cup ketchup
1 tablespoon prepared mustard
1 large clove garlic, minced

Dash hot pepper sauce
½ teaspoon salt
Generous dash pepper
1 small green pepper, cut into
    1-inch squares
1½ cups thickly sliced
    mushrooms (about ¼ pound)
Tomato wedges

In skillet, brown meat in shortening; pour off fat. Add broth, water, onion, ketchup, mustard, garlic, hot pepper sauce, and seasonings. Cover; cook over low heat 2 hours. Add green pepper and mushrooms; cook 30 minutes more or until meat is tender. Stir occasionally. Thicken if desired. Garnish with tomato. Makes about 4 cups.

❋ Roast Beef El Capitan
Pictured on front cover

4-pound rolled rib roast
½ cup cooked ham strips
2 medium cloves garlic, minced

1 can (10¾ ounces) condensed
    golden mushroom soup
⅓ cup water
1 teaspoon capers (optional)

Place meat, fat-side up, in large roasting pan. Roast at 325°F. for 2 hours 20 minutes or until desired doneness (rare — about 35 minutes per pound or 140°F. on meat thermometer). Remove meat from pan; pour off excess fat, saving drippings. On top of range, in roasting pan, brown ham with garlic in drippings. Add soup; stir to loosen browned bits. Add water and capers. Heat; stir occasionally. After slicing meat, add meat juices to gravy. 6 servings.

❋ Best Ever Meat Loaf

1 can (10¾ ounces) condensed
    cream of mushroom or golden
    mushroom soup
2 pounds ground beef
½ cup fine dry bread crumbs

⅓ cup finely chopped onion
1 egg, slightly beaten
1 teaspoon salt
⅓ cup water

Mix thoroughly ½ cup soup, beef, bread crumbs, onion, egg, and salt. Shape *firmly into loaf* (8x4 inches); place in shallow baking pan. Bake at 375°F. for 1 hour 15 minutes. In saucepan, blend remaining soup, water, and 2 to 3 tablespoons drippings. Heat; stir occasionally. Serve with loaf. 6 to 8 servings.

Frosted Meat Loaf: Prepare loaf as above; bake for 1 hour. Frost loaf with 4 cups mashed potatoes; sprinkle with shredded Cheddar cheese. Bake 15 minutes more.

Swedish Meat Loaf: Add ½ teaspoon nutmeg to loaf. Blend remaining soup with ⅓ cup sour cream; omit drippings and water. Serve over loaf; sprinkle with additional nutmeg. Garnish with thinly sliced cucumber.

Meat Loaf Wellington:
Crescent Rolls *(Refrigerated):* Prepare loaf as above. Bake at 375°F. for 1 hour. Spoon off fat. Separate 1 package (8 ounces) refrigerated crescent dinner rolls; place crosswise over top and down sides of meat loaf, overlapping slightly. Bake 15 minutes more.

Patty Shells: Thaw 1 package (10 ounces) frozen puff pastry patty shells. Prepare loaf as above. Bake at 375°F. for 30 minutes. Spoon off fat. Increase oven temperature to 400°F. On floured board, roll 5 patty shells into rectangle (12x8 inches); prick several times with fork. Cover top and sides of loaf with pastry. Decorate top with remaining patty shell, rolled and cut into fancy shapes. Bake for 45 minutes more or until golden brown. Serve with sauce.

Perfect Pot-Luck Casserole

1 pound ground beef
⅓ cup chopped onion
1 cup shredded Cheddar cheese
1 can (10¾ ounces) condensed
    tomato soup

2 cups cooked medium noodles
1 cup cooked corn
¼ cup water
1 teaspoon prepared mustard
1 teaspoon salt

In saucepan, brown beef and cook onion until tender; stir to separate meat. Pour off fat. Stir in ¾ cup cheese and remaining ingredients. Spoon into 1½-quart casserole. Bake at 350°F. for 30 minutes or until hot; stir. Top with remaining cheese. Bake until cheese melts. Makes about 5 cups.

Green Bean: Substitute 1 cup cooked cut green beans for corn.

A simplified version of the classic Beef Wellington is
Meatloaf Wellington *made quickly with refrigerated crescent rolls.*
Doubly good with Golden Mushroom Sauce.

❋ *Super Rolled Meat Loaf*

2 cans (10¾ ounces each)
  condensed cream of mushroom
  soup
3 pounds ground beef
½ cup finely chopped onion
2 cups small bread cubes
2 eggs, slightly beaten
8 slices (8 ounces) boiled ham

8 slices (8 ounces) Swiss cheese
½ medium green pepper, cut in
  strips
Generous dash tarragon
1 tablespoon butter or margarine
⅓ cup water
½ cup chopped canned tomatoes

Combine 1 cup soup, beef, onion, bread cubes, and eggs. *Mix thoroughly*. Divide in half. On waxed paper, pat into two 12x9-inch pieces. Press ham and cheese into each to within 1 inch of edges. With aid of waxed paper, roll meat tightly jelly-roll fashion starting at long edges. Seal ends; use waxed paper to transfer to shallow baking dishes. Bake at 350°F. for 1 hour. Meanwhile, in saucepan, cook green pepper with tarragon in butter until tender. Add remaining soup, water, and tomatoes. Heat; stir occasionally. Serve with loaves. 12 servings.

❋ *Many Way Meatballs*

1 pound ground beef
¼ cup fine dry bread crumbs
¼ cup finely chopped onion
1 egg, slightly beaten
¼ teaspoon salt

1 can (11 ounces) condensed
  Cheddar cheese, cream of
  celery or mushroom, golden
  mushroom, tomato or
  vegetable soup
2 to 4 tablespoons water
2 tablespoons chopped parsley

Mix beef, bread crumbs, onion, egg, and salt; shape into 16 meatballs. In skillet, brown meatballs; pour off fat. Stir in soup, water, and parsley. Cover; cook over low heat 20 minutes or until done. Stir occasionally. Makes about 3½ cups.

Ring Meat Loaf with Tomato-Cheese Topping

6 slices bacon
½ cup finely chopped onion
1 can (10¾ ounces) condensed
  tomato soup
1½ pounds ground beef
½ cup fine dry bread crumbs
  or 1 cup cooked rice

¼ cup chopped parsley
1 egg, slightly beaten
⅛ teaspoon pepper
2 slices (2 ounces) process
  cheese, split diagonally

In skillet, cook bacon until crisp; remove and crumble. Cook onion in 2 tablespoons bacon drippings until tender. Mix thoroughly with ½ can soup, beef, crumbs, parsley, egg, bacon, and pepper. In shallow baking dish (13x9x2 inches), shape firmly into ring (2 inches high with 4-inch opening). Bake at 350°F. for 1 hour. Spoon off fat. Top ring with remaining soup and cheese; bake until cheese starts to melt. Remove ring with the aid of two spatulas. 6 servings.

Deluxe Crusty Meat Loaf

Pastry for 2-crust pie
1½ pounds ground beef
1 can (10¾ ounces) condensed
  cream of celery soup
1 cup cooked rice
1 egg, slightly beaten
½ cup finely chopped onion
¼ cup finely chopped parsley
1 teaspoon salt
½ teaspoon tarragon, crushed
Generous dash pepper
1 cup sliced mushrooms (about ¼
  pound)
1 small clove garlic, minced
2 tablespoons butter or margarine
¼ cup milk
2 tablespoons Madeira

Roll pastry into a rectangle (16x11 inches). Combine beef, ¼ cup soup, rice, egg, onion, parsley, salt, tarragon, and pepper. Lengthwise on pastry, lightly shape beef mixture into loaf (11x3 inches). Cover entire loaf with pastry by overlapping and sealing long edges on top of loaf. Fold up ends and seal. Turn loaf seamside down on well-greased baking sheet or shallow baking dish; brush with milk. Make several slits on top and sides of loaf. Bake at 375°F. for 1 hour. Remove, using 2 spatulas. Meanwhile, in saucepan, cook mushrooms and garlic in butter until tender. Add remaining soup, milk, and Madeira. Heat; stir occasionally. Serve with loaf. 6 servings.

❋ *Skillet Meat Loaf*

1 can (10¾ ounces) condensed
  tomato soup
1½ pounds ground beef
½ cup fine dry bread crumbs
1 egg, slightly beaten
¼ cup finely chopped onion
1 teaspoon salt
Generous dash pepper
1 tablespoon shortening
¼ cup water
½ teaspoon prepared mustard
2 slices (2 ounces) process
  cheese, cut in half

Combine ¼ cup soup with meat, bread crumbs, egg, onion, salt, and pepper; mix *thoroughly*. Shape *firmly* into 2 loaves. In skillet, brown loaves in shortening. Cover; cook over low heat 25 minutes. Spoon off fat. Stir in remaining soup, water, and mustard. Top loaves with cheese. Cook *uncovered* 10 minutes. Stir occasionally. 6 servings.

Oven Method: Shape loaves as above. Place in a shallow baking pan. Bake at 350°F. for 40 minutes. Spoon off fat. Pour remaining soup (omit water) mixed with mustard over loaves. Top with cheese. Bake 5 minutes more.

Liver 'n Beans Piquant

4 slices bacon
1½ pounds sliced beef or calf's
   liver
2 tablespoons flour
1 can (11 ounces) condensed
   tomato bisque soup

¾ cup water
1 package (10 ounces) frozen
   cut green beans, cooked and
   drained
⅛ teaspoon garlic salt

In skillet, cook bacon until crisp; remove. Pour off all but 2 tablespoons drippings. Dust liver with flour; brown in bacon drippings. Add soup, water, beans, and garlic salt. Cover; cook over low heat 20 minutes or until tender. Stir occasionally. Garnish with bacon. 6 servings.

Old favorite foods, like friends, are ever-appealing. This adaptation of an Irish Boiled Dinner *will start lots of eyes a'smiling for St. Patrick's or any other dinner.*

Irish Boiled Dinner

4-pound brisket corned beef
1 can (10½ ounces) condensed
    onion soup
4 whole peppercorns
1 medium clove garlic, minced
1 bay leaf
¼ teaspoon rosemary, crushed
6 medium carrots, cut in
    1½-inch pieces

6 medium potatoes, quartered
½ cup celery cut in 1-inch
    pieces
1 medium head green cabbage,
    cut in wedges
3 tablespoons water
3 tablespoons flour

Rinse corned beef. Place in large heavy pan; add soup and seasonings. Cover; cook over low heat for 3½ hours. Add carrots, potatoes, and celery. Place cabbage on top. Cover; cook about 1 hour or until all ingredients are tender. Remove meat, vegetables, and bay leaf. Gradually blend water into flour until smooth; slowly stir into sauce. Cook, stirring until thickened. 6 to 8 servings.

Stuffed Peppers

4 medium green peppers
1 pound ground beef
½ cup chopped onion
1 can (10¾ ounces) condensed
    tomato soup
1 cup cooked rice

2 teaspoons Worcestershire
½ teaspoon salt
Generous dash pepper
2 slices (2 ounces) mild process
    or Swiss cheese, cut in strips

Remove tops and seeds from peppers; cook in boiling salted water about 5 minutes; drain. In skillet, brown beef and cook onion until tender; stir in 1 cup soup, rice, and seasonings. Spoon meat mixture into peppers; place in 1½-quart casserole. Bake at 375°F. for 25 minutes. Top with remaining soup and cheese. Bake 5 minutes more. 4 servings.

Spanish Rice with Beef

1 pound ground beef
½ cup chopped green pepper
½ cup chopped onion
1 large clove garlic, minced
1 can (10¾ ounces) condensed
    tomato soup

1½ cups water
1½ cups quick-cooking rice,
    uncooked*
1 tablespoon Worcestershire
½ teaspoon salt
Generous dash pepper

In saucepan, brown beef and cook green pepper and onion with garlic until tender; stir to separate meat. Add remaining ingredients. Bring to a boil; reduce heat. Cover; cook over low heat 5 minutes or until done. Stir occasionally. Makes about 5 cups.

*If desired, substitute ⅓ cup raw regular rice for quick-cooking rice; reduce to 1 cup water. Cook over low heat 30 minutes or until rice is tender.

❊ Stuffed Cabbage Rolls

8 large cabbage leaves
1 can (10¾ ounces) condensed
    tomato soup
1 pound ground beef
1 cup cooked rice

¼ cup chopped onion
1 egg, slightly beaten
1 teaspoon salt
¼ teaspoon pepper

Cook cabbage in salted water a few minutes to soften; drain. Mix 2 tablespoons soup with remaining ingredients. Divide meat mixture among cabbage leaves; fold in sides and roll up (secure with toothpicks, if necessary). In skillet, place rolls seam side down; pour remaining soup over. Cover; cook over low heat for 40 minutes. Stir occasionally, spooning sauce over rolls. 4 servings.

❈ Stuffed Flank Provencale

1½-pound flank steak
1½ cups cooked rice or 1½ cups
   cooked fine noodles
½ cup grated Parmesan cheese
2 tablespoons melted butter
2 tablespoons shortening
1 can (10¾ ounces) condensed
   golden mushroom soup

1 can (10¾ ounces) condensed
   tomato soup
½ cup chopped onion
1 large clove garlic, minced
½ teaspoon basil, crushed
½ teaspoon oregano, crushed

An increasingly popular lean cut flank steak comes about ¾ inch thick and is superb when stuffed.

Pound steak until thin. Combine rice, Parmesan, and butter. Spread mixture evenly on steak to within 1 inch of edges. Starting at narrow end, roll up; tuck in ends. Tie with string or fasten with skewers. In skillet, brown roll in shortening; pour off fat. Add remaining ingredients. Cover; cook over low heat 1 hour. Turn; cook 1 hour more or until tender. Stir occasionally. 6 to 8 servings.

❈ Tamale Casserole

1 pound ground beef
½ cup chopped onion
1 large clove garlic, minced
1 tablespoon chili powder
⅛ teaspoon ground cumin

1 can (10¾ ounces) condensed
   tomato soup
½ cup sliced ripe olives
1 can (about 16 ounces)
   prepared tamales

In skillet, brown meat and cook onion with garlic, chili powder, and cumin until tender; stir to separate meat. Add soup and olives. Pour into shallow baking dish (10x6x2 inches). Remove tamales from wrappers; arrange on top. Bake at 350°F. for 20 minutes or until hot. 4 servings.

Beef Souffle

1 can (10¾ ounces) condensed
   cream of mushroom soup
½ cup shredded sharp Cheddar
   cheese
½ teaspoon marjoram, crushed

Dash cayenne
1 cup finely chopped cooked
   beef or veal
2 tablespoons chopped parsley
6 eggs, separated

In saucepan, combine soup, cheese, and seasonings. Heat slowly until cheese melts. Remove from heat; stir in beef and parsley. Beat egg yolks until thick and lemon-colored; stir into soup mixture. In large bowl, beat egg whites until soft peaks are formed; fold soup mixture into egg whites. Pour into ungreased 2-quart casserole. Bake at 300°F. for 1¼ hours or until done. Serve immediately. 4 to 6 servings.

❊ *Teriyaki*

In Japan yaki dishes are skewered foods which are generally broiled over charcoal braziers. They may be made with fish, poultry or game, but beef most commonly. For added pleasure, cook the meat on a hibachi.

1½ pounds boneless sirloin steak (1-inch thick)
1 can (10½ ounces) condensed beef broth
¼ cup soy sauce
¼ cup diagonally sliced green onions

1 large clove garlic, minced
1 tablespoon brown sugar
¼ teaspoon ground ginger
Cooked rice

Freeze meat 1 hour to firm (makes slicing easier); slice into *very* thin strips. Combine remaining ingredients except rice; pour over steak. Marinate 2 hours. Thread meat on 4 skewers. Broil about 4 inches from heat until desired doneness (5 to 10 minutes), brushing with marinade and turning once. Heat remaining marinade; thicken if desired. Serve with meat and rice. 4 servings.

Beef Roulades Royale

1½ pounds thinly sliced round steak (¼-inch thick)
½ pound finely ground veal
1 egg
2 tablespoons finely chopped onion
2 tablespoons finely chopped parsley
⅛ teaspoon nutmeg

Generous dash pepper
6 thin carrot sticks
6 thin celery sticks
2 tablespoons shortening
1 can (11 ounces) condensed Cheddar cheese soup
½ cup chopped tomatoes

Cut steak into 6 pieces (about 6x4 inches); pound. Thoroughly mix veal, egg, onion, parsley, and seasonings; divide into sixths. Place veal mixture on narrow end of meat; top with carrot and celery stick. Roll steak; secure with toothpicks or skewers. In skillet, brown roll-ups in shortening. Pour off fat. Add soup and tomatoes. Cover; cook over low heat 1 hour 15 minutes or until meat is tender. Stir occasionally. 6 servings.

Steak Lyonnaise

1 pound round steak (½-inch thick)
2 tablespoons shortening
1 can (10¾ ounces) condensed cream of celery soup

¼ cup water
1 cup sliced onion
½ teaspoon Worcestershire
1 large clove garlic, minced
1 medium tomato, cut in wedges

Pound steak; cut into serving-size pieces. In skillet, brown steak in shortening; pour off fat. Add soup, water, onion, Worcestershire, and garlic. Cover; cook over low heat 1½ hours or until tender. Stir occasionally. Add tomato wedges; heat. 4 servings.

Saucy Steak with Parsnips

1½ pounds round steak (½-inch
    thick), cut in 1-inch squares
2 tablespoons shortening
1 can (10¾ ounces) condensed
    cream of mushroom soup
1 can (10½ ounces) condensed
    beef broth

½ cup water
¼ cup brandy
2 tablespoons chopped pimiento
⅛ teaspoon marjoram, crushed
⅛ teaspoon thyme, crushed
1 pound parsnips, cut in 1-inch
    pieces (about 2 cups)

In skillet, brown round steak in shortening; pour off fat. Add remaining ingredients except parsnips. Cover; cook over low heat 1 hour. Add parsnips; cook 30 minutes more or until tender. Stir occasionally. 4 to 6 servings.

London Broil with Mushroom-Tomato Sauce

1½-pound top quality flank steak
½ cup sliced onion
1 tablespoon butter or margarine
1 can (10¾ ounces) condensed
    golden mushroom soup

⅓ cup water
⅓ cup chopped canned tomatoes
2 tablespoons chopped parsley
1 tablespoon Dijon mustard

Broil meat 2 inches from heat 5 minutes on each side. Meanwhile, in saucepan, cook onion in butter until tender. Add remaining ingredients. Heat; stir occasionally. Thinly slice meat diagonally across the grain. Serve with sauce. 6 servings.

Chop Soupy

1 pound boneless round
    steak (¾-inch thick)
1½ cups diagonally sliced celery
1 medium green pepper, cut in
    1-inch pieces
1½ cups sliced fresh mushrooms
    (about ¼ pound)

½ cup diagonally sliced green
    onions (1-inch pieces)*
2 tablespoons salad oil
1 can (10½ ounces) condensed
    beef broth or onion soup
1 tablespoon soy sauce
2 tablespoons cornstarch
Cooked rice

Freeze meat 1 hour to firm (makes slicing easier); slice into *very* thin strips. In skillet, cook celery, pepper, mushrooms, and onion in oil until *just* tender; push to one side. Add meat; cook until color changes. Add broth, soy, and cornstarch. Cook, stirring until thickened. Serve with rice and additional soy sauce. Makes about 4½ cups.

*Omit onions when using onion soup

❈ Meatballs Oriental

1 pound ground beef
1 cup small bread cubes
1 egg, slightly beaten
1/4 cup finely chopped onion
1/2 teaspoon salt
1/4 teaspoon ground allspice
1 can (12 ounces) pineapple
   chunks in pineapple juice

1 can (10½ ounces) condensed
   beef broth
1/3 cup sliced water chestnuts
1/4 teaspoon ground ginger
2 tablespoons cornstarch
1 small green pepper, diced
Cooked rice

Great cooks create some of their greatest successes by developing a palate for seasonings....Experiment with herbs, spices, condiments, fruit juices, vinegars and flavoring extracts for your own specialties.

Mix *thoroughly* beef, bread cubes, egg, onion, salt, and 1/8 teaspoon allspice. Drain pineapple, saving juice. Shape beef *firmly* around 16 pineapple chunks to form 16 meatballs. In skillet, brown meatballs (use shortening if necessary); pour off fat. Stir in broth, 1/4 cup pineapple juice, water chestnuts, ginger, and remaining pineapple chunks and allspice. Cover; cook over low heat 20 minutes. Stir occasionally. Combine remaining pineapple juice and cornstarch. Slowly stir into sauce; add green pepper. Cook, stirring until thickened and green pepper is done. Serve with rice. Makes about 4½ cups.

❈ Chinese Pepper Steak

1 pound boneless round steak
   (¾-inch thick)
1 large green pepper, cut
   into strips
2 tablespoons salad oil

1 can (10½ ounces) condensed
   onion soup
1/2 cup chopped canned tomatoes
2 tablespoons cornstarch
1 tablespoon soy sauce
Cooked rice

Freeze meat 1 hour to firm (makes slicing easier); slice into *very* thin strips. In skillet, cook green pepper in oil until just tender; push to one side. Add meat; cook until color changes. Add soup, tomatoes, cornstarch, and soy. Cook, stirring until thickened. Serve with rice and additional soy. Makes about 4 cups.

❈ Easy Pot Roast

3 to 4-pound beef pot roast
1 can (10½ ounces) condensed

onion, golden mushroom, or
   cream of mushroom soup

In large heavy pan, brown meat on all sides (use shortening if necessary). Pour off fat. Stir in soup. Cover; cook over low heat 2½ to 3 hours. Stir occasionally. Remove meat. To thicken, gradually blend 1/4 cup water into 2 to 4 tablespoons flour. Slowly stir into soup. Cook, stirring until thickened. 6 to 8 servings.

Superb for buffet parties are Meatballs Oriental *and* Chinese Pepper Steak, *both served with rice. Each sauce is spicy and slightly sweet.*

Swiss Steak

1/4 cup flour
1/2 teaspoon salt
Generous dash pepper
1 1/2 pounds round steak
   (3/4-inch thick)

2 tablespoons shortening
1 can (10 3/4 ounces) condensed
   vegetable soup
1/2 soup can water
1 cup sliced onions

Combine flour and seasonings; pound into steak. Cut steak into serving-size pieces. In skillet, brown steak in shortening; pour off fat. Add remaining ingredients. Cover; cook over low heat 1 1/2 hours or until tender. Stir occasionally. 4 to 6 servings.

❋ Beef Stroganoff

1 pound boneless round
   steak (3/4-inch thick)
1/2 cup chopped onion
2 tablespoons butter or margarine

1 can (10 3/4 ounces) condensed
   golden mushroom
   or cream of mushroom soup
1/2 cup sour cream
1/4 cup water
1/2 teaspoon paprika
Cooked noodles

Freeze meat 1 hour to firm (makes slicing easier); slice into *very* thin strips. In skillet, cook onion in butter until *just* tender; push to one side. Add meat; cook until color changes. Add remaining ingredients except noodles. Heat; stir occasionally. Serve over noodles. Makes about 3 1/2 cups.

❋ Beef Bourguignonne

4 slices bacon
2 pounds sirloin beef cubes
   (about 1 1/2 inches)
2 cans (10 1/2 ounces each)
   condensed beef broth
1 cup Burgundy or other dry
   red wine
1 large clove garlic, minced
1/2 teaspoon thyme, crushed

4 medium carrots, cut in half
1/2 pound (about 8) small whole
   white onions
2 cups sliced fresh mushrooms
   (about 1/2 pound)
1/3 cup water
1/4 cup flour
Cooked noodles or rice
Chopped parsley

In large, heavy, oven-proof pan, cook bacon until crisp; remove and crumble. Brown beef in drippings; pour off fat. Add crumbled bacon, soup, wine, garlic, and thyme. Cover; bake at 350°F. for 1 hour 15 minutes. Add carrots, onions, and mushrooms. Bake 45 minutes more or until meat and vegetables are tender. Gradually blend water into flour until smooth; slowly stir into sauce. Cook, stirring until thickened. Serve over noodles or rice; garnish with parsley. Makes about 7 cups.

❋ Beef Roll-Ups

1½ cups herb seasoned stuffing
1½ pounds thinly sliced round
    steak (¼-inch thick)
2 tablespoons shortening

1 can (10¾ ounces) condensed
    golden mushroom soup
¼ cup water
Parsley

Prepare stuffing as directed on package. Cut meat into 6 pieces (8x4 inches); pound. Place about ¼ cup stuffing near center of each piece of meat. Starting at narrow end, roll up. Tuck in ends; fasten with toothpicks or skewers. In skillet, brown roll-ups in shortening; pour off fat. Stir in soup and water. Cover; cook over low heat 1 hour 15 minutes or until tender. Stir occasionally. Garnish with parsley. 6 servings.

❋ Spread-a-Burger

1 can (10¾ ounces) condensed
    tomato soup
1 tablespoon prepared mustard
1 tablespoon Worcestershire
1 teaspoon prepared horseradish
1½ pounds ground beef

⅓ cup finely chopped onion
1 teaspoon salt
Generous dash pepper
6 long hard rolls or frankfurter
    buns, slit and lightly toasted
Sliced process cheese

Combine soup, mustard, Worcestershire, and horseradish. Mix *thoroughly* ⅓ cup soup mixture, beef, onion, salt, and pepper. Spread mixture evenly on buns; *cover edges completely.* Bake at 400°F. for 10 minutes. Top with remaining soup mixture and cheese; bake 5 minutes more. Makes 6 sandwiches.

Glazed Cold Platter

1 envelope unflavored gelatine
½ cup cold water
1 can (10½ ounces) condensed
    consomme
¼ cup Madeira
2 teaspoons grated onion

5 slices cooked tongue
10 slices cooked beef
1 can (16 ounces) whole baby
    carrots, drained
1 hard-cooked egg, sliced
2 stuffed olives, sliced

In saucepan, sprinkle gelatine on cold water to soften. Place over low heat, stirring until gelatine is dissolved. Remove from heat; stir in soup, wine, and onion. Chill until slightly thickened. Meanwhile, on a large serving platter (13x9 inches), arrange overlapping slices of tongue and beef. Garnish with carrots and egg topped with olives. Spoon a thin layer of gelatine mixture over the entire platter. Chill until set. 5 servings.

A decorated cold platter deserves the place of honor at your buffet table. This is a much-simplified twentieth-century version of the fanciful aspics made famous by Careme and other French chefs.

Chuck with Herb-Anchovy Sauce

3-pound boned chuck roast
  (about 2-inches thick)
1 can (10¾ ounces) condensed
  cream of celery soup
½ cup chopped onion
⅓ cup chopped canned tomatoes

1 medium clove garlic, minced
½ teaspoon tarragon, crushed
1 can (2 ounces) rolled
  anchovy fillets stuffed with
  capers

Trim fat from meat; place in shallow baking dish (12x8x2 inches). Roast at 350°F. for 1 hour; spoon off fat. Combine remaining ingredients except anchovies. Pour over meat. Cover with foil; bake 2 hours more or until tender. Spoon off fat. Top roast with anchovies. 6 servings.

❊ Chuck and Potato Bake

3½-pound boned chuck roast
  (about 2-inches thick)
6 medium potatoes (about 2
  pounds), peeled and cut in
  half

2 cans (10¾ ounces each)
  condensed cream of
  mushroom soup
1 tablespoon chopped dried
  chives, optional
½ cup grated Cheddar cheese
Paprika

Trim fat from meat; place in large baking pan (13x9x2 inches). Roast at 350°F. for 1 hour; spoon off fat. Arrange potatoes around roast. Combine soup and chives; pour over meat and potatoes. Cover with foil; bake 2 hours more or until meat and potatoes are tender. Sprinkle with cheese and paprika; bake until cheese melts. 6 servings.

❊ Roast Chuck Neopolitan

3½-pound boned chuck roast
  (about 2-inches thick)
2 tablespoons shortening
1 can (10¾ ounces) condensed
  tomato soup

½ cup water
1 cup sliced onion
1 large clove garlic, minced
2 teaspoons oregano, crushed
Generous dash pepper

In large heavy pan, brown meat in shortening. Pour off fat. Stir in remaining ingredients. Cover; cook over low heat 2½ hours or until tender. Spoon off fat. Thicken sauce if desired. 6 servings.

When preparing herbs you will achieve more flavor from the dry variety by chopping it with a fresh one. For example, try combining fresh parsley and dried tarragon or oregano.

Two popular foods combine in **Chuck and Potato Bake** *with an easy-to-make cheese sauce. Delectable fare for the family or an informal company supper.*

Braised Short Ribs with Dumplings

3 pounds short ribs, cut in
   serving-size pieces
2 tablespoons shortening
1 can (10¾ ounces) condensed
   cream of celery soup
1 can (10½ ounces) condensed
   onion soup
1 can (16 ounces) tomatoes,
   cut up

½ cup water
2 tablespoons Worcestershire
2 large cloves garlic, minced
1 medium bay leaf
1 pound carrots, cut in 2-inch
   pieces (about 2 cups)
1½ cups biscuit mix
1 teaspoon ground savory
½ cup milk

Trim excess fat from ribs. In Dutch oven, brown ribs in shortening; pour off fat. Stir in soups, tomatoes, water, Worcestershire, garlic, and bay. Cover; cook over low heat 1 hour 45 minutes. Stir occasionally. Add carrots. Cover; cook 1 hour more. Spoon fat off surface, if necessary. Combine biscuit mix and savory; stir in milk. Drop 8 spoonfuls onto boiling stew; cook 10 minutes. Cover; cook 10 minutes more. Serve immediately. 4 servings.

Beef Caribe

4 slices bacon
1½ pounds beef cubes (1½ inches)
1 can (10¾ ounces) condensed
   tomato soup
1 soup can water
1 cup chopped onion
2 medium bay leaves

1 teaspoon paprika
Dash crushed red pepper
4 medium potatoes (about 1½ pounds),
   quartered
1 cup chopped green pepper
½ cup pitted ripe olives
1 tablespoon drained capers

In large heavy pan, cook bacon until crisp; remove and crumble. In drippings, brown beef. Add soup, water, onion, bay leaves, paprika, red pepper, and bacon. Cover; cook over low heat 1 hour 45 minutes. Stir occasionally. Add potatoes. Cook 30 minutes more. Add green pepper, olives, and capers. Cook 15 minutes more or until tender. Remove bay leaves. Makes about 7 cups.

Creamed Horseradish Sauce on Cooked Beef

2 eggs, slightly beaten
1 tablespoon milk
Salt and pepper
4 servings sliced cooked beef
2 tablespoons flour
1/4 cup fine dry bread crumbs
2 tablespoons butter or margarine

1 can (10¾ ounces) condensed
   cream of mushroom soup
1/4 cup milk
2 teaspoons prepared
   horseradish
1/2 teaspoon dried dill leaves,
   crushed

Combine eggs, 1 tablespoon milk, salt, and pepper. Dip slices of beef in flour, then egg mixture, then crumbs. In skillet, brown beef in butter. Meanwhile, in saucepan, combine remaining ingredients. Heat; stir occasionally. Serve sauce over beef. 4 servings.

Tacos

1½ cups chopped cooked beef
1/2 cup chopped onion
2 large cloves garlic, minced
1 tablespoon chili powder
2 tablespoons salad oil

1 can (10¾ ounces) condensed
   tomato soup
8 tortillas
Grated Cheddar cheese
Shredded lettuce
Chopped avocado

In saucepan, brown beef and cook onion with garlic and chili powder in oil until onion is tender. Add soup. Heat; stir occasionally. In skillet, cook one tortilla at a time in hot oil for an instant until it is pliable; remove. Place about 1/4 cup meat mixture in center of tortilla; top with cheese, lettuce, and avocado. Fold tortilla in half. Makes 8 tacos.

Ground Beef: Substitute 1 pound ground beef for cooked beef; omit salad oil. Proceed as above. Makes about 10 tacos.

❋ Swedish Chuck Stew

3½-pound boned chuck roast
   (about 2-inches thick)
2 tablespoons shortening
2 cans (10¾ ounces each)
   condensed cream of mushroom
   soup
1/2 cup sour cream

1/2 cup water
1 teaspoon paprika
Generous dash pepper
1 pound medium carrots, halved
1 pound small whole white
   onions
Cooked wide noodles

Trim fat from meat and cut into 1-inch cubes. In large heavy pan, brown beef in shortening; pour off fat. Add soup, sour cream, water, paprika, and pepper. Cover; cook over low heat 1 hour. Add vegetables. Cook 1 hour more or until meat and vegetables are tender. Stir occasionally. Thicken sauce if desired. Serve with noodles. Makes about 8 cups.

PORK·VEAL LAMB

Beef may be king, but pork, veal, lamb and variety meats also rank high in the culinary peerage. Readily available, they bring versatility to your table for family meals, holiday celebrations or that particular occasion which calls for something special.

Pork was greatly cherished in early America, not only because it was good eating and nutritious, but because it could be easily preserved — salted, smoked or made into sausages. As our second most popular meat today, it is greatly appreciated for its rich diversity. Fresh or cured, we have chops, roasts, steaks, butts, hocks and tenderloins. There are spareribs, picnic hams, sausages and the renowned frankfurter.

The texture and taste of veal are entirely different from the meat of mature beef. Because it is so lean, veal should be cooked with the addition of fat, and is generally braised, roasted, stewed, or gently fried. Veal takes to seasoning and combines particularly well with piquant flavors.

Many of our best veal dishes are adaptations from European creations and are excellent party main dishes. For an epicurean meal, feature veal delicately flavored with a superb sauce.

A fine-textured meat with distinctive, appealing flavor, lamb is becoming more appreciated in America. Long esteemed as important fare for special feasts in Europe and the Middle East, it earns its reputation as an elegant entree for company meals.

Lamb has a particular affinity for sauces and stuffings. It is also compatible with a wide range of interesting foods and seasonings which make the various dishes especially attractive. Among the best of them are the delicious stews, casseroles, roasts, patties and increasingly popular skewered shish kabobs.

Meat 'n Biscuit Bake

Plan a cosy oven supper for a wintry eve — and serve this homey casserole. Before you put in the meat dish, bake cinnamon-rosy apples for dessert.

1 cup biscuit mix
¼ cup water
2 tablespoons grated Parmesan cheese
1½ cups cubed cooked beef
⅓ cup chopped onion

½ teaspoon oregano leaves, crushed
2 tablespoons butter or margarine
1 can (10¾ ounces) condensed golden mushroom soup
1 cup cooked cut green beans
½ cup chopped canned tomatoes

To make biscuits, combine biscuit mix and water; mix as directed on package. Roll into 8-inch square; sprinkle with cheese. Roll up jelly-roll fashion; cut into 8 slices. Meanwhile, in saucepan, brown beef and cook onion with oregano in butter until tender. Stir in soup, beans, and tomatoes; bring to boil. Pour into 1½-quart casserole. Place biscuits around edge of casserole. Bake at 450°F. for 15 minutes or until hot. Makes about 3½ cups.

❋ Country-Fried Pork Chops

6 pork chops (about 1½ pounds)
1 can (10¾ ounces) condensed cream of celery soup
⅓ cup water
1 cup thinly sliced carrots

1 can (about 2 ounces) sliced mushrooms, drained
¼ teaspoon thyme, crushed
1 can (16 ounces) small whole white onions, drained

In skillet, brown chops (use shortening if necessary); pour off fat. Stir in soup, water, carrots, mushrooms, and thyme. Cover; cook over low heat 30 minutes or until done. Stir occasionally. Add onions; heat. 4 servings.

Texas Pork Chops

1 can (11¼ ounces) condensed chili beef soup
¾ cup cooked rice
2 tablespoons finely chopped green pepper
2 tablespoons sliced ripe olives

4 thick pork chops (about 1½ pounds)
1 can (16 ounces) tomatoes, chopped and drained
1 medium onion, sliced
1 medium clove garlic, minced

Combine ¼ cup soup, rice, green pepper, and olives. Trim excess fat from chops. Slit each chop from outer edge toward bone making a pocket; stuff with rice mixture. Fasten with toothpicks or skewers. In skillet, brown chops (use shortening if necessary); pour off fat. Add remaining ingredients. Cover; cook over low heat 1¼ hours or until done. Stir occasionally. 4 servings.

❈ Pork Chops Charcutiere

6 pork chops (about
   1½ pounds)
1 can (10¾ ounces) condensed
   golden mushroom soup
¼ cup water

⅓ cup chopped onion
2 teaspoons prepared mustard
2 tablespoons sweet or dill gherkin
   pickles cut in strips

In skillet, brown chops; pour off fat. Add soup, water, onion, and mustard. Cover; cook over low heat 30 minutes or until tender. Stir occasionally. Add pickles. 4 servings.

❈ Pork Chops a l'Orange

8 rib pork chops (about 2 pounds)
Pepper
2 cans (10¾ ounces each) condensed
   cream of chicken soup
½ cup fresh orange juice

½ cup diagonally sliced celery
¼ cup coarsely chopped cashews
Generous dash ground cloves
8 fresh orange slices, cut in half

Use 1 large skillet or prepare in 2 skillets (about 10 inches), by dividing ingredients equally. Brown chops (use shortening if necessary); pour off fat. Season with pepper. Stir in remaining ingredients except orange slices. Cover; cook over low heat 25 minutes. Stir occasionally. Add orange slices. Cook over low heat 5 minutes more or until done. 6 servings.

❈ Ham 'n Turkey Casserole

2 cups ham strips
1 teaspoon poultry seasoning
1 tablespoon butter or margarine
2 cans (10¾ ounces each)
   condensed cream of celery
   soup
⅔ cup milk
2 cups cubed cooked turkey

1 can (16 ounces) small whole
   white onions, drained
1 package (10 ounces) frozen
   peas, cooked and drained
2 packages (8 ounces each)
   refrigerated crescent dinner rolls
1 package (8 ounces) sliced
   process cheese or ½ cup
   shredded Cheddar cheese

In saucepan, brown ham with poultry seasoning in butter. In shallow baking dish (13x9x2 inches), combine ham with remaining ingredients except rolls and cheese. Bake at 400°F. for 20 minutes or until hot. Meanwhile, cut cheese slices diagonally in half. Separate rolls. Top each roll with cheese triangle. Roll up as directed on package. Stir hot casserole; top with rolls. Bake 15 to 20 minutes more or until rolls are done. 8 servings.

Stuffed Chops and Yams

1/3 cup chopped celery
1 cup diced apple
1/4 cup raisins
1/2 teaspoon paprika
2 tablespoons butter or
    margarine
4 thick pork chops
    (about 1 1/2 pounds)

1 can (10 3/4 ounces) condensed
    golden mushroom soup
1/2 cup sour cream
1/4 cup water
1 can (16 ounces) sweet
    potatoes, drained

In saucepan, cook celery with apple, raisins, and 1/4 teaspoon paprika in butter until tender. Trim excess fat from chops. Slit each chop from outer edge toward bone making a pocket; stuff with apple mixture. Fasten with toothpicks or skewers. In skillet, brown chops (use shortening if necessary); pour off fat. Stir in soup, sour cream, water, and remaining 1/4 teaspoon paprika. Cover; cook over low heat 1 hour. Add potatoes; cook 15 minutes more or until done. Stir occasionally. 4 servings.

Chops 'n Cabbage Skillet

6 pork chops (about 1 1/2 pounds)
1 can (10 3/4 ounces) condensed
    cream of celery soup
1/3 cup water
1/2 cup chopped onion

1 teaspoon caraway seed
Generous dash pepper
4 cabbage wedges, 2 inches
    wide (about 1 pound)

In skillet, brown chops (use shortening if necessary); pour off fat. Stir in soup, water, onion, caraway, and pepper. Arrange cabbage on top of chops. Cover; cook over low heat 30 minutes or until done. Stir occasionally. 4 servings.

Saucy Pork Chops

6 pork chops (about 1 1/2 pounds)
Salt
Pepper
1 can (10 3/4 ounces) condensed
    tomato soup

1/4 cup water
6 onion slices
6 green pepper rings

In skillet, brown chops (use shortening if necessary); pour off fat. Season with salt and pepper. Stir in soup and water. Top each chop with onion and green pepper. Cover; cook over low heat 30 minutes or until tender. Stir occasionally. 4 servings.

Flavorful Stuffed Chops and Yams *with a mushroom sauce becomes a superb supper. Cook and serve in the same attractive skillet.*

Pork with Shrimp

*1 pound boneless loin of pork,
  cut in very thin strips*
2 tablespoons salad oil
*1 can (10¾ ounces) condensed
  tomato soup*
*1 pound medium shrimp (about
  18), cleaned and cut in half
  lengthwise*

¼ cup water
*2 tablespoons finely chopped
  chutney*
*2 tablespoons chopped green
  pepper*
1 tablespoon lemon juice
Generous dash ground coriander

In skillet, brown pork in oil. Add remaining ingredients. Cover; cook over low heat 10 minutes or until pork and shrimp are done. Stir occasionally. Serve with hot fluffy rice. Makes about 4½ cups.

Baked Spareribs with Sauerkraut

*4 pounds spareribs, cut in
  serving-size pieces*
Pepper
*1 can (10½ ounces) condensed
  onion soup*

*1 can (27 ounces)
  sauerkraut, drained*
1½ cups shredded apple
1 teaspoon caraway seed

Sprinkle spareribs with pepper; arrange fat side up in shallow baking pan (14x10x2 inches). Bake at 325°F. for 1½ hours turning once. Remove ribs; pour off fat. Combine remaining ingredients in pan; top with ribs. Bake 1½ hours more. 4 servings.

Roast Pork Party-Style

3-pound loin of pork
6 slices onion
*3 slices apple, cut in half
  (¼-inch thick)*
¼ teaspoon sage

*1 can (10¾ ounces) condensed
  cream of chicken soup*
¼ cup Madeira or sherry
⅓ to ½ cup water

Make 6 slits almost to bone in pork loin. Place a slice of onion and ½ slice apple in each slit. Rub roast with sage. Tie securely. Roast fat side up at 325°F. for 2 hours. Pour off fat. Combine soup and Madeira; pour over meat. Roast 30 minutes more or until done, basting often with soup (total roasting time takes 35 to 40 minutes per pound or 170°F. on meat thermometer). Remove meat from pan. On top of range, in roasting pan, add water to soup. Heat, stirring to loosen browned bits. Serve with roast. 4 to 6 servings.

Veal Chops Roma

6 veal chops (about 1½ pounds)
1 medium clove garlic, minced
½ teaspoon oregano, crushed
3 tablespoons butter or margarine

1 can (10¾ ounces) condensed
  tomato soup
½ cup sliced onion
1 cup green pepper strips
½ cup sliced ripe olives

In skillet, brown chops and cook garlic with oregano in butter. Add soup and onion. Cover; cook over low heat 30 minutes. Add pepper and olives. Cook 15 minutes more or until done. Stir occasionally. 4 servings.

❊ Veal Scallopine Marsala

1½ pounds thinly sliced veal
  tenders
¼ cup butter or margarine
¼ cup Marsala wine

1 can (10½ ounces) condensed
  beef broth
1 tablespoon flour

Cut veal into 3-inch pieces; pound. In skillet, brown veal in butter. Add wine. Bring to boil; stir to loosen browned bits. Gradually blend broth into flour until smooth. Slowly stir into skillet. Cook, stirring until thickened. 6 servings.

Veal Birds with Polenta

1½ pounds thinly sliced veal
  cutlet
6 thin slices proscuitto (Italian
  ham)
2 slices (about 3 ounces) Mozzarella cheese, cut in 6 pieces
2 tablespoons butter or margarine
2 tablespoons chopped onion

1 medium clove garlic, minced
1 can (10¾ ounces) condensed
  cream of mushroom soup
⅓ cup milk
4 cups water
1 cup cornmeal
1 teaspoon salt

Once upon a time a luxurious Italian dish was roasted small birds and polenta. Over the years thin slices of meat, stuffed and rolled up, became known as "poor men's birds" which are now regal fare.

Cut veal into 6 pieces (about 6x4 inches); pound. Place 1 slice proscuitto on each piece veal; top with cheese. Roll up; fasten with toothpicks. In skillet, brown roll-ups in butter; push to side and cook onion with garlic until tender. Stir in soup and milk. Cover; cook over low heat 45 minutes or until tender. Stir occasionally. Meanwhile, mix 1 cup water, cornmeal, and salt; pour into 3 cups boiling water, stirring constantly. Cook until thickened, stirring often. Cover; cook over low heat for 25 minutes. Spoon mush around edge of platter; arrange roll-ups in center. 6 servings.

Cranberry Glazed Ham with Sauce

5-pound canned ham
¾ cup jellied cranberry sauce
1 can (10½ ounces) condensed
   consomme

½ cup applesauce
1 tablespoon cornstarch
1 teaspoon lemon juice
Generous dash allspice

In shallow baking pan, bake ham at 325°F. for 1 hour. Pour off fat. Score; spread ¼ cup cranberry sauce over top. Bake 30 minutes more (18 minutes per pound or 140°F. on meat thermometer). Remove to platter. In baking pan, combine remaining ingredients. Cook, stirring constantly until thickened. Pour some sauce over ham; serve remainder. 8 to 10 servings.

Veal Roast South Pacific

¼ cup softened butter or
   margarine
2 to 3 teaspoons curry powder
1 large clove garlic, minced
3-pound veal roast (rump)

1 can (10¾ ounces) condensed
   cream of celery soup
½ cup sour cream
⅓ cup water
½ cup drained pineapple
   tidbits

Combine butter, curry, and garlic. Spread on top and sides of veal. Roast at 325°F. for 2 hours or until done (35 to 40 minutes per pound or 170°F. on meat thermometer). Remove veal from pan. Pour off fat, saving drippings. On top of range, in roasting pan, blend soup and sour cream into drippings. Add water and pineapple. Heat, stirring to loosen browned bits. Serve with roast. 6 servings.

Creamed Sweetbreads Olivero

1 pound sweetbreads
½ cup sliced onion
1 medium clove garlic, minced
2 tablespoons butter or margarine
1 can (10¾ ounces) condensed
   cream of mushroom soup

⅓ cup milk
⅓ cup chopped canned
   tomatoes
¼ cup sliced stuffed olives
Cooked rice

For a party, precook sweetbreads (lamb, veal or beef); then cube and brown them with seasonings before the guests arrive. Add remaining prepared ingredients minutes before serving.

In saucepan, combine 1 quart water, 1 teaspoon salt, and 1 tablespoon lemon juice. Bring to a boil. Add sweetbreads. Cover; cook over low heat 20 minutes. Drain; remove membrane. Cut sweetbreads into cubes. In saucepan, brown sweetbreads and cook onion and garlic in butter until onion is tender. Add soup, milk, tomatoes, and olives. Heat; stir occasionally. Serve over rice. Makes about 3 cups.

Planning to feature ham for a buffet party? Everyday canned ham becomes an elegant entree as Cranberry Glazed Ham.

✳ Sunday Best Veal Rolls

1 cup chopped onion
1/4 cup butter or margarine
1/2 cup chopped parsley
1 1/2 pounds thinly sliced veal cutlet

1 can (10 3/4 ounces) condensed
  cream of celery soup
1 teaspoon grated lemon rind
Whipped potatoes
Frosted grapes
Lemon wedges

In skillet, cook onion in 2 tablespoons butter until tender; add parsley. Cut veal into 6 pieces (about 6x4 inches); pound. Place about 1 tablespoon onion mixture on each piece of veal; roll up and fasten with toothpicks or skewers. In same skillet, brown veal in remaining butter. Add soup. Cover; cook over low heat 45 minutes or until tender. Stir occasionally. Add rind. Serve with potatoes; garnish with grapes and lemon. 6 servings.

✳ Veal Saltimbocca

8 thin slices veal cutlet
  (about 1 1/2 pounds)
1/4 teaspoon rubbed sage
8 thin slices (about 4 ounces)
  prosciutto or boiled ham

2 tablespoons butter or
  margarine
1/2 cup Chablis or other
  dry white wine
1 can (10 3/4 ounces) condensed
  golden mushroom soup

Pound veal; rub with sage. Place slice of ham on each piece; fasten with toothpicks. In skillet, brown veal in butter. Add wine; bring to boil. Stir to loosen browned bits. Simmer a few minutes. Stir in soup; heat. 6 servings.

✳ Blanquette de Veau

This famous French dish is a rich ragout or stew made with veal or chicken, mushrooms and onions. It is named for its creamy white sauce.

1 can (10 3/4 ounces) condensed
  chicken broth
2 pounds veal cubes
  (about 1 1/2 inches)
2 tablespoons chopped parsley
1 small clove garlic, minced
1 teaspoon lemon juice
1/2 teaspoon thyme, crushed

Generous dash ground cloves
1 pound (about 16) small
  whole white onions
2 cups small fresh mushroom
  caps (about 1/2 pound)
3/4 cup light cream
3 tablespoons flour
Cooked rice

In skillet, combine broth, veal, parsley, garlic, lemon juice, thyme, and cloves. Cover; cook over low heat 1 hour. Add onions and mushrooms. Cook 30 minutes more or until meat and vegetables are tender. Gradually blend cream into flour until smooth; slowly stir into sauce. Cook, stirring until thickened. Serve with rice. Makes about 6 cups.

❋ *Veal Chasseur*

1 pound thinly sliced veal, cut
   into serving-size pieces
2 tablespoons butter or margarine
1 can (10¾ ounces) condensed
   golden mushroom soup
¼ cup water

½ cup chopped canned
   tomatoes
4 small whole white onions
2 tablespoons white wine
¼ teaspoon chervil leaves

Pound veal. In skillet, brown veal in butter; add remaining ingredients. Cover; cook over low heat 20 minutes or until tender. Stir occasionally. 4 servings.

Lamb Breast, Sausage Stuffing

1 pound sausage
1 cup chopped celery
1 large clove garlic, minced
1 package (8 ounces) herb
   seasoned stuffing
1 can (10½ ounces) condensed
   onion soup

2 breasts of lamb with pocket
   for stuffing (about 2 pounds
   each)
2 teaspoons rosemary, crushed
1 can (10¾ ounces) condensed
   cream of mushroom soup
⅓ cup water
¼ cup chopped chutney

In skillet, brown sausage and cook celery with garlic. Add stuffing and 1 cup onion soup. Toss lightly. Spoon ½ stuffing into each breast; fasten with skewers. Rub each breast with 1 teaspoon rosemary. Roast at 325°F. for 1 hour 15 minutes or until done (35 to 40 minutes per pound or 175°F. on meat thermometer). Remove meat from pan. Pour off fat, saving drippings. On top of range, in roasting pan, add mushroom soup, water, chutney, and remaining onion soup. Heat, stirring to loosen browned bits. Serve with roast. 6 servings.

Lamb 'n Rice Skillet

1½ pounds lamb cubes (about
   1 inch), well-trimmed
2 tablespoons shortening
1 can (10½ ounces) condensed
   beef broth
½ cup sliced onion

1 medium clove garlic, minced
¼ teaspoon thyme, crushed
⅔ cup raw regular rice
1 package (10 ounces)
   frozen peas
¼ cup cashews

In skillet, brown lamb in shortening; pour off fat. Add broth, onion, garlic, and thyme. Cover; cook over low heat 30 minutes. Add rice and peas. Cook 25 minutes more or until lamb and rice are tender. Stir occasionally. Add cashews. Makes about 4 cups.

Lamb Chops in Spicy Sauce

4 shoulder lamb chops (about
   1½ pounds), trimmed
½ cup cubed ham
1 tablespoon shortening
1 can (10¾ ounces) condensed
   tomato soup

½ cup sliced onion
¼ cup water
⅛ teaspoon nutmeg
Generous dash mace, optional
Buttered noodles

In skillet, brown chops and ham in shortening; pour off fat. Add remaining ingredients except noodles. Cover; cook over low heat 45 minutes or until chops are tender. Stir occasionally. Serve with noodles. 4 servings.

Quick Cutlets Italiano

½ cup chopped onion
1 large clove garlic, minced
¼ teaspoon oregano, crushed
⅛ teaspoon thyme, crushed
2 tablespoons butter or margarine
1 can (10¾ ounces) condensed
   tomato soup
½ cup water

1 can (12 ounces) luncheon
   meat, cut in 8 slices
1 egg, slightly beaten
½ cup bread crumbs
2 tablespoons shortening
2 slices (3 ounces)
   Mozzarella cheese
Grated Parmesan cheese

In saucepan, cook onion with garlic, oregano, and thyme in butter until tender. Stir in soup and water; cook over low heat 15 minutes. Stir occasionally. Meanwhile, dip luncheon meat slices in egg, then in bread crumbs. In skillet, brown meat on one side in shortening; turn and pour sauce over. Top with Mozzarella; sprinkle with Parmesan. Cover; heat until cheese melts (about 3 minutes). 4 servings.

Lamb Indienne

1½ pounds lamb cubes
   (about 1½ inches)
2 tablespoons shortening
1 can (10¾ ounces) condensed
   cream of chicken soup
½ cup sliced onion

¼ cup water
1 large clove garlic, minced
1 tablespoon curry powder
1 cup diced apple
Cooked rice

In skillet, brown lamb in shortening; pour off fat. Add soup, onion, water, garlic, and seasonings. Cover; cook over low heat 1½ hours. Stir occasionally. Add apple the last 5 minutes. Serve with rice; garnish with chopped chutney, toasted coconut, raisins. Makes about 4 cups.

A treasured foreign food is **Lamb Indienne,** *a subtly seasoned curried dish. Serve over rice. Let guests help themselves to the attractive and toothsome tidbits for garnish.*

Canadian Bacon and Yam Bake

1 can (about 13 ounces)
    pineapple chunks in heavy syrup
1 cup green pepper strips
2 tablespoons butter or margarine
1 can (10½ ounces) condensed
    beef broth
2 tablespoons cornstarch

2 tablespoons honey
2 teaspoons lemon juice
½ teaspoon dry mustard
1 can (16 ounces) sweet potatoes,
    drained
1 pound Canadian bacon, cut into
    8 slices

Drain pineapple reserving ⅓ cup syrup. In saucepan, cook green pepper in butter until tender. Stir in soup, reserved pineapple syrup, cornstarch, honey, lemon juice, and mustard. Cook, stirring constantly until thickened. In 1½-quart casserole, arrange alternate layers of potatoes, bacon, pineapple, and sauce. Cover; bake at 350°F. for 45 minutes. 4 servings.

❋ Frankfurter Crown Casserole

2 slices bacon
1 cup chopped onion
1 can (10¾ ounces) condensed
    cream of mushroom soup
⅓ cup water
2 tablespoons vinegar
½ teaspoon salt

⅛ teaspoon pepper
4 cups sliced cooked potatoes
1 package (10 ounces) frozen cut
    green beans, cooked and drained
½ pound frankfurters, cut in
    half lengthwise and crosswise

In skillet, cook bacon until crisp; remove and crumble. Cook onion in drippings until tender. Stir in soup, water, vinegar, salt, and pepper; add potatoes and green beans. Pour into 1½-quart casserole. Bake at 400°F. for 30 minutes or until hot; stir. Stand frankfurters around edge of casserole. Bake 10 minutes more. Garnish with bacon. Makes 4 servings.

The art of making sausages is one of the world's oldest ways of preparing meats. The word derives from the Latin for salt. Many of our varieties came from Europe but early colonists excelled in sausage making.

Sausage 'n Noodles Napoli

½ pound sausage links,
    cut in 1-inch pieces
½ pound Italian sausage,
    cut in 1-inch pieces
1 can (about 4 ounces) sliced
    mushrooms, drained
½ cup chopped celery

1 can (10½ ounces) condensed
    onion soup
¾ to 1 cup water
½ cup chopped canned
    tomatoes
2 cups uncooked fine noodles
1 package (10 ounces)
    frozen peas

In skillet, brown sausages. Add mushrooms and celery; cook until tender. Pour off fat. Add remaining ingredients. Bring to boil. Cover; cook over low heat 10 minutes or until done. Stir often. Makes about 6½ cups.

Skillet Frankaroni

6 frankfurters, slashed
1/2 cup chopped green pepper
1/2 cup chopped onion
1 teaspoon chili powder
1/4 cup butter or margarine
1 can (11 ounces) condensed
   Cheddar cheese soup

1/2 cup water
2 cups cooked elbow macaroni
1 package (9 ounces) frozen
   cut green beans, cooked and
   drained

In skillet, brown frankfurters and cook pepper and onion with chili powder in butter until tender. Stir in soup and water. Add macaroni and beans. Heat; stir occasionally. 3 to 4 servings.

Sausage-Apple Bake

1 pound bulk sausage
1 cup shredded apple
1/3 cup fine dry bread crumbs
1/4 cup finely chopped onion
1 egg, slightly beaten
Generous dash pepper
2 cans (10 1/2 ounces each)
   condensed beef broth

1/4 cup water
1 1/2 cups sliced carrots
   (1/2-inch thick)
1/8 teaspoon mace
1 cup raw regular rice
3 apple slices (1/2-inch thick),
   cut in half

Combine sausage, apple, crumbs, onion, egg, and pepper; mix thoroughly. Shape into 16 meatballs. In oven-proof skillet, brown meatballs; pour off fat. Stir in broth, water, carrots, and mace. Bring to boil; stir in rice. Cover; bake at 450°F. for 15 minutes. Stir; arrange apple pieces between meatballs. Cover; bake 10 minutes more or until rice is tender. Makes about 5 cups.

Bologna Bundles

1 can (11 1/2 ounces) condensed
   bean with bacon soup
1/3 cup chopped dill pickle
1 tablespoon grated onion

1 pound bologna, cut into
   1/4-inch thick slices
1/2 cup shredded Cheddar
   cheese
Paprika

Combine soup, pickle, and onion; place equal amounts soup mixture on each slice bologna. Fold over; fasten with toothpicks or skewers. Arrange in shallow baking dish (12x8x2 inches). Bake at 350°F. for 20 minutes. Sprinkle with cheese and paprika; bake 10 minutes more. 4 servings.

SEAFOOD

The world of seafood is fascinating to contemplate and pleasurable to explore. And our country is blessed with a wide variety of foods from the sea. Available fresh, frozen or canned, we can offer seafood to our family and friends as a welcome change of pace. In one form or another, fish and shellfish can make a menu memorable.

Without these denizens of the sea, the American colonists might not have survived. In those early days, and for many decades thereafter, our forefathers were limited to seafood in season or those which had been preserved. Generally they were acquainted with only those in their own or nearby locales. However, this did not hinder the creation of many superb seafood dishes which have become classics of the American table.

Among these excellent regional specialties are New England's seafood and clam chowders, oyster stew, codfish cakes and fried clams. In the Middle Atlantic states cooks prepare native crabs and oysters in many ways and are fond of baked stuffed rockfish and seafood pies. In the South there are such famous delights as baked red snapper, Creole gumbo, jambalaya and stuffed crabs. Westerners are fond of their salmon steaks, Dungeness crabs and delectable cioppino.

Fortunately, everyone can now enjoy at least some of these regional specialties and many other seafood dishes. Modern progress in canning, freezing and transportation makes much of the nation's seafood bounty available everywhere and at any time of the year.

Cooking seafood is not difficult, just remember that it should not be overcooked or the precious juices will be lost.

Seafood is an excellent choice when entertaining. Weight conscious guests will appreciate that it is low in calories and high in nutritive value.

❊ *Fish Bonne Femme*

1½ pounds fillet of sole or flounder
1 cup sliced fresh mushrooms (about ¼ pound)
2 tablespoons finely chopped onion
2 tablespoons chopped parsley

½ cup Chablis or other dry white wine
1 can (10¾ ounces) condensed cream of celery soup
¼ cup heavy cream, whipped

In skillet, place sole on bottom; top with mushrooms, onion, and parsley. Add wine. Cover; cook over low heat 10 minutes. Carefully transfer fish and garnish to oven-proof platter. Stir soup into ¼ cup of the remaining liquid; heat. Fold in whipped cream. Pour over fish. Place under broiler until lightly browned. 6 servings.

Fillet of Sole Veronique: Omit mushrooms, onion, and parsley from above recipe. Substitute 1 cup seedless white grapes.

❊ *Perfect Tuna Casserole*

1 can (10¾ ounces) condensed cream of celery or mushroom soup
¼ cup milk
1 can (about 7 ounces) tuna, drained and flaked

2 hard-cooked eggs, sliced
1 cup cooked peas
½ cup slightly crumbled potato chips

In 1-quart casserole, blend soup and milk; stir in tuna, eggs, and peas. Bake at 350°F. for 25 minutes; stir. Top with chips; bake 5 minutes more or until hot. Makes about 4 cups.

Easy Tuna Rice

⅓ cup chopped onion
2 tablespoons butter or margarine
1 can (10¾ ounces) condensed chicken broth
1½ cups quick-cooking rice, uncooked

¼ cup sliced water chestnuts
1 teaspoon soy sauce
1 can (about 7 ounces) tuna, drained and flaked
1 cup cooked Italian green beans

In saucepan, cook onion in butter until tender. Add broth, rice, chestnuts, and soy. Bring to a boil. Cover; cook over low heat about 5 minutes or until all liquid is absorbed. Add tuna and beans; heat. Serve with additional soy. Makes about 4 cups.

Favorite Curried Tuna

1/4 cup sliced green onions
1 teaspoon curry powder
2 tablespoons butter or margarine
1 can (10 3/4 ounces) condensed
   cream of chicken soup
1/3 cup milk

1/2 cup chopped unpeeled apple
1/4 cup toasted slivered
   almonds
1 can (about 7 ounces) tuna,
   drained and flaked
Patty shells

In saucepan, cook onions with curry in butter until tender. Stir in remaining ingredients except patty shells. Heat; stir occasionally. Serve in patty shells. Makes about 2 1/2 cups.

❊ Famous Seafood Stew

2 lobster tails (about 1/2 pound)
1 cup sliced onion
1 medium clove garlic, minced
2 tablespoons butter or margarine
1 can (10 3/4 ounces) condensed
   Manhattan style clam chowder
1 can (10 3/4 ounces) condensed
   New England clam chowder

1/2 cup water
1/4 cup Chablis or other dry
   white wine
1 pound scallops
2 tablespoons chopped parsley
1 pound white fish, cut in
   2-inch pieces

Remove lobster meat from shells; cut up. In large pan, cook onion with garlic in butter until tender. Add remaining ingredients except fish. Cook over low heat 5 minutes; add fish. Cook 5 minutes more or until fish is done. Stir occasionally. Makes about 8 cups. If desired, before serving stew, place in each bowl a slice of Italian bread fixed this way. (Spread with butter, sprinkle with crushed dill; bake at 450°F. for 10 minutes).

Gourmet Shrimp

1/4 cup chopped green onions
2 tablespoons butter or
   margarine
1 can (10 3/4 ounces) condensed
   cream of mushroom soup

1/4 cup light cream
2 pounds medium shrimp
   (about 36), cleaned
2 tablespoons chopped parsley
2 tablespoons cognac

In skillet, cook onion in butter until tender. Add remaining ingredients. Cover; simmer 10 minutes or until shrimp is done. Stir occasionally. Makes about 4 1/2 cups.

❋ Crab Louis

1 can (10¾ ounces) condensed
   cream of celery soup
½ cup chili sauce
¼ cup mayonnaise
2 tablespoons finely
   chopped onion
Generous dash pepper

¼ cup heavy cream, whipped
4 cups cooked flaked crab meat
   (about 1½ pounds)
Hard-cooked egg, cut in wedges
Tomatoes, cut in wedges

Blend soup, chili, mayonnaise, onion, and pepper; fold in whipped cream. Add crab; chill. Place crab on bed of lettuce. Garnish with egg and tomato. Makes about 4 cups.

Swordfish with Cucumber Sauce

2 teaspoons anchovy paste
6 tablespoons softened
   butter or margarine
6 swordfish steaks
   (about 1½ pounds)
1 cup diced cucumber
½ teaspoon dried dill weed,
   crushed

2 tablespoons butter
   or margarine
1 can (10¾ ounces)
   condensed cream of
   mushroom soup
⅓ cup sour cream

Cream anchovy paste and softened butter; spread on steaks. Broil 4 inches from heat for 5 minutes on each side or until fish flakes easily. Meanwhile, in saucepan, cook cucumber with dill in butter until tender. Add soup and sour cream. Heat; stir occasionally. Serve over fish. 6 servings.

Little Salmon Loaves with Mushroom Sauce

2 cans (7½ ounces each)
   salmon, drained and flaked
1 can (10¾ ounces) condensed
   cream of mushroom soup
1 egg, slightly beaten
½ cup finely chopped onion
¼ cup fine dry bread crumbs

2 teaspoons prepared
   horseradish
½ teaspoon prepared mustard
¼ cup sour cream
2 tablespoons water
¼ cup chopped canned
   tomatoes
2 teaspoons chopped chives

In bowl, combine salmon, ¼ cup soup, egg, onion, crumbs, horseradish, and mustard. Mix well. Pack into well-buttered individual molds or custard cups (6-ounce size). Bake at 350°F. for 20 minutes. Unmold. Meanwhile, combine remaining ingredients. Heat; stir occasionally. Serve over salmon. 4 servings.

*Two prized fruits of the sea with inventive sauces, Crab Louis
and Swordfish with Cucumber Sauce.*

Lobster Cantonese

½ pound ground pork
2 medium cloves garlic, minced
¼ cup vegetable oil
1½ pounds raw lobster, cut in
   bite-size pieces
1 can (10¾ ounces) condensed
   chicken broth
1 soup can water

½ cup diagonally sliced
   green onions
2 tablespoons soy sauce
Generous dash pepper
3 tablespoons cornstarch
¼ cup water
1 egg, slightly beaten

In skillet, cook pork and garlic in oil until done; stir. Add lobster, soup, water, onions, soy, and pepper. Cook over low heat 2 to 3 minutes or until lobster is done. Mix cornstarch and ¼ cup water; gradually add to sauce. Cook, stirring until thickened. Stir egg into sauce. Makes about 6 cups.

There are numerous fine foods to serve in attractive individual sea shells or baking dishes. Two of them are Crab au Gratin and Coquille St. Jacques, superb luncheon fare.

Crab au Gratin

1 cup sliced mushrooms
   (about ¼ pound)
¼ cup chopped onion
¼ teaspoon marjoram, crushed
2 tablespoons butter or margarine
1 can (10¾ ounces) condensed
   cream of celery soup

1 tablespoon sherry
1 can (7 ounces) crab,
   drained and flaked
¼ cup shredded Swiss cheese
Paprika

In saucepan, brown mushrooms and cook onion with marjoram in butter until tender. Stir in soup, sherry, and crab. Heat; stir occasionally. Spoon into 4 individual seashells or baking dishes. Sprinkle with cheese and paprika. Broil until cheese melts. 4 servings.

❋ Broiled Lobster Tails au Gratin
Pictured on back cover

4 lobster tails (about 2 pounds)
½ cup sliced green onions
¼ teaspoon chervil, crushed
2 tablespoons butter or margarine

1 can (10¾ ounces)
   condensed cream of
   mushroom soup
¼ cup sour cream
½ cup shredded Cheddar
   cheese

Cook lobster tails in boiling water for 10 minutes or until done. Remove meat (keeping shells intact); cut in 1-inch pieces. In saucepan, cook onion with chervil in butter until tender. Add soup, sour cream, and lobster. Heat; stir occasionally. Spoon lobster mixture into shells. Top with cheese. Broil 4 to 5 inches from heat until cheese melts. 4 servings.

❋ Coquille St. Jacques

1½ pounds scallops
2 cups sliced mushrooms
   (about ½ pound)
2 tablespoons sliced green
   onions
¼ cup butter or margarine

1 can (10¾ ounces) condensed
   cream of celery soup
⅓ cup Chablis or other dry
   white wine
2 tablespoons chopped parsley
¼ cup buttered bread crumbs

In saucepan, cook scallops in water over low heat for 10 minutes; drain well. Meanwhile, in saucepan, cook mushrooms and green onions in butter until tender. Add soup, wine, parsley, and scallops. Heat; stir occasionally. Spoon into 6 individual baking dishes. Top with crumbs. Place under broiler until lightly browned. 6 servings.

Lobster Continental on Rice

1 whole chicken breast (about
   ¾ pound), split, skinned, and
   boned
⅛ teaspoon tarragon, crushed
2 tablespoons butter or margarine
2 cans (11 ounces each)
   condensed Cheddar cheese soup
⅔ cup milk

⅓ cup sherry
2 cups cubed cooked lobster
1 package (9 ounces) frozen
   artichoke hearts, cooked and
   drained
½ cup chopped canned tomatoes
3 cups cooked rice
¼ cup chopped watercress

Cut chicken into strips. In skillet, brown chicken with tarragon in butter. Stir in soup, milk, and sherry. Add lobster, artichokes, and tomatoes. Heat; stir occasionally. Meanwhile, combine rice and watercress. Serve lobster mixture over rice. Makes about 7 cups.

Tempting Seafood Casserole

½ cup chopped celery
¼ cup chopped onion
2 tablespoons chopped green
   pepper
2 tablespoons butter or margarine
1 can (10¾ ounces) condensed
   cream of mushroom soup

¼ cup water
2 cups diced cooked lobster or
   shrimp
1 teaspoon lemon juice
½ cup shredded mild
   process cheese
2 tablespoons buttered bread
   crumbs

In saucepan, cook celery, onion, and pepper in butter until tender. Add remaining ingredients except cheese and crumbs. Pour into 1-quart casserole. Bake at 400°F. for 20 minutes; stir. Top with cheese and crumbs. Bake 5 minutes more or until hot. Makes about 3 cups.

❋ Flounder Florentine

¼ cup chopped onion
⅛ teaspoon rosemary, crushed
2 tablespoons butter or margarine
1 package (9½ ounces) frozen
   chopped spinach, cooked and
   well-drained
½ cup cooked rice
¼ cup chopped toasted almonds

1 tablespoon lemon juice
6 fresh fillets of flounder
   (about 1½ pounds)
1 can (10¾ ounces) condensed
   cream of mushroom soup
¼ cup water
Paprika

In saucepan, cook onion with rosemary in butter until tender. Add spinach, rice, almonds, and lemon juice. Heat; stir occasionally. Place ¼ cup mixture on each fish fillet. Roll; secure with toothpicks. Arrange in shallow baking dish (12x8x2 inches). Bake at 350°F. for 20 minutes. Meanwhile, blend soup and water; pour over fish, stirring around sides. Bake 15 minutes more or until done. Stir sauce before serving. Sprinkle with paprika. 6 servings.

A welcome change of pace for fish fanciers, Flounder Florentine has a stuff
of almonds, spinach and rice. Generously ladled over all, creamy mushroom sau

Cioppino

½ cup chopped green pepper
½ cup chopped onion
2 medium cloves garlic, minced
¼ teaspoon oregano, crushed
Generous dash crushed thyme
¼ cup olive oil
2 cans (10¾ ounces each)
    condensed tomato soup
1 cup water

½ cup Sauterne or other dry
    white wine
1 pound medium shrimp
    (about 18), cleaned
2 lobster tails (½ pound),
    cracked
2 tablespoons chopped parsley
1 medium bay leaf
1 pound fillets of haddock,
    cut in 2-inch pieces

In large pan, cook green pepper, onion, garlic, oregano, and thyme in oil until vegetables are tender. Add remaining ingredients except haddock. Cook over low heat 10 minutes. Add haddock; cook 10 minutes more. Stir gently now and then. Remove bay leaf. Makes about 8½ cups.

POULTRY

Our domesticated fowl — chicken, turkey, duckling and Rock Cornish hens — rate high as choice entrees for entertaining. They have universal appeal, exceptional flavor and versatility. Once luxury fare, poultry is now a favorite for all seasons and all occasions.

It was Henry IV of France who promised his people a chicken in every pot, or *poule au pot,* and who did a great deal to popularize the bird. But the globe-trotting chicken, native to Southeast Asia, traversed the world to become important in every cuisine.

Early Americans took pride in presenting chicken for company dinners, particularly on Sunday. They served it fried, smothered, barbecued, baked, roasted, creamed, made into pie, shortcake, fricassee, *a la* King or Brunswick stew. Every table of any epicurian worth featured one or more kinds of chicken.

Moderate in calories and high in protein, chicken comes fresh, frozen or canned. Contributing greatly to its ease of preparation are the readily available chicken parts which do not require much handling before cooking.

Turkey, a gift of the New World to the Old, has been associated traditionally with winter holiday meals. It holds a place of honor at Thanksgiving and Christmas tables, but is now appearing more regularly on year-round menus. Available in various sizes, turkey is perfect either for little meals or large get-togethers. It is excellent for buffets and, cooked on a spit, favored for outdoor dining.

Of our domesticated fowl, the old-favorite duckling and the newer Rock Cornish hen, are a pleasure to serve because they have the virtue of being unusual. Both are generally roasted, broiled or grilled outdoors. Many excellent stuffings and sauces may be served with them, and they blend well with fruit and sweet-sour flavorings.

❋ Bombay Chicken

2 pounds chicken parts
2 tablespoons shortening
1 can (10¾ ounces) condensed
   tomato soup
⅓ cup water
¼ cup chopped onion

1 medium clove garlic, minced
1 teaspoon curry powder
¼ teaspoon thyme, crushed
Toasted slivered almonds,
   flaked coconut, chutney,
   sliced green onions, and raisins

In skillet, brown chicken in shortening; pour off fat. Add soup, water, onion, garlic, curry, and thyme. Cover; cook over low heat 45 minutes or until chicken is tender. Stir occasionally. Serve with a variety of the remaining ingredients. 4 servings.

❋ Chicken Marengo

3 pounds chicken parts
3 tablespoons shortening
1 can (10¾ ounces) condensed
   golden mushroom soup

1 can (10¾ ounces) condensed
   tomato soup
1 medium clove garlic, minced
1 pound (about 16) small whole
   white onions

In large skillet, brown chicken in shortening; pour off fat. Stir in remaining ingredients. Cover; cook over low heat 45 minutes or until tender. Stir occasionally. Uncover; cook until desired consistency. 6 servings.

Chicken Basque

Chicken Basque acquires its name from a "region" in northwest Spain and southwest France where cooking is a dedicated art. The traditional fine ingredients combine to make a marvelous company casserole.

3 pounds chicken parts
2 tablespoons shortening
Salt and pepper
2 cans (10¾ ounces each)
   condensed tomato soup
¼ cup Chablis or other dry
   white wine

4 cups eggplant strips, ¾ inch
   thick (1 large eggplant)
½ pound mushrooms, quartered
½ cup diced cooked ham
½ cup chopped green pepper
2 medium cloves garlic, minced
⅛ teaspoon pepper
1 medium bay leaf

In large skillet, brown chicken in shortening. Transfer to 3-quart casserole; sprinkle with salt and pepper. Pour off fat in skillet; stir in soup and wine. Mix in remaining ingredients; pour over chicken. Cover; bake at 350°F. for 1 hour. Remove bay leaf. 6 servings.

Popular Chicken Marengo is ingeniously flavored with the twosome of magical golden mushroom and tomato soups. It's an economical recipe, attractive and savory

❊ *Glorified Chicken*

2 pounds chicken parts
2 tablespoons shortening

1 can (10¾ ounces) condensed
Cheddar cheese, cream of celery,
chicken, or mushroom soup

In skillet, brown chicken in shortening. Pour off fat. Stir in soup. Cover; cook over low heat 45 minutes or until tender. Stir occasionally. 4 servings.

Oven Method: In shallow baking dish (12x8x2 inches), arrange chicken skin-side down. Pour 2 tablespoons butter over. Bake at 400°F. for 20 minutes. Turn chicken; bake 20 minutes more. Stir soup; pour over chicken. Bake 20 minutes more or until tender. Stir sauce before serving.

❊ *Chicken Crunch*

1 can (10¾ ounces) condensed
cream of chicken, mushroom,
*or golden mushroom soup ***
¾ cup milk
1 tablespoon finely chopped
onion

1 tablespoon chopped parsley
2 pounds chicken parts
1 cup finely crushed packaged
herb seasoned stuffing
2 tablespoons melted butter or
margarine

Mix ⅓ cup soup, ¼ cup milk, onion, and parsley. Dip chicken in soup mixture; then roll in stuffing. Place in shallow baking dish (12x8x2 inches). Drizzle butter on chicken. Bake at 400°F. for 1 hour or until tender. Meanwhile, combine remaining soup and milk. Heat; stir occasionally. Serve over chicken. 4 servings.

*When using golden mushroom soup, substitute water for milk.

Wine imparts a desirable subtle flavor to a dish and during the cooking the alcohol evaporates. The better the wine the better the dish. Use sparingly. Add after the poultry or meat has been browned.

❊ *Coq au Vin*

2 pounds chicken parts
2 tablespoons shortening
1 can (10¾ ounces) condensed
chicken broth
1 can (about 4 ounces) whole
mushrooms, drained
⅓ cup Burgundy or other dry
red wine

10 small whole white onions
(about ½ pound)
1 medium bay leaf
1 large clove garlic, minced
¼ teaspoon thyme, crushed
½ cup water
¼ cup flour

In skillet, brown chicken in shortening; pour off fat. Add broth, mushrooms, wine, onions, bay, garlic, and thyme. Cover; cook over ~~low heat~~ 45 minutes or until chicken and onions are tender. Stir occasionally. Remove bay leaf. Gradually blend water into flour until smooth; slowly stir into sauce. Cook, stirring until thickened. 4 servings.

❋ *Tetrazzini*

2 tablespoons chopped onion
1 tablespoon butter or margarine
1 can (10¾ ounces) condensed
   cream of mushroom soup
½ cup water
½ cup shredded sharp Cheddar
   cheese

1 tablespoon sherry, optional
1 cup diced cooked chicken, turkey, or ham
2 tablespoons chopped pimiento
1 tablespoon chopped parsley
2 cups cooked spaghetti

In saucepan, cook onion in butter until tender. Blend in soup, water, cheese, and sherry. Heat until cheese melts; stir occasionally. Add chicken, pimiento, parsley, and spaghetti; heat. Makes about 3½ cups.

❋ *Chicken Cacciatore*

2 pounds chicken parts
2 tablespoons shortening
1 can (10¾ ounces) condensed
   tomato soup
½ cup chopped onion
¼ cup Chianti or other dry red wine

2 large cloves garlic, minced
½ teaspoon oregano, crushed
⅛ teaspoon salt
½ medium green pepper, cut
   into strips

In skillet, brown chicken in shortening; pour off fat. Add remaining ingredients except pepper. Cover; cook over low heat 30 minutes. Add pepper. Cook 15 minutes more or until chicken is tender. Stir occasionally. 4 servings.

❋ *Chicken Via Veneto*

4 pounds chicken parts
¼ cup butter or margarine
1 cup ham strips, optional
2 cans (11 ounces each)
   condensed Cheddar cheese soup

½ cup chopped canned tomatoes
3 medium onions, quartered
½ teaspoon basil, crushed

Use 1 large skillet or prepare in 2 skillets (about 10 inches) by dividing ingredients equally. Brown chicken in butter; remove. Brown ham. Stir in soup, tomatoes, onions, and basil; add chicken. Cover; cook over low heat 45 minutes or until tender. Stir occasionally. 8 servings.

Pages 82-83: Three gifts from Italy: Via Veneto, Tetrazzini *and* Chicken Cacciatore *are triumphant main dishes for entertaining. Offer with any of them, a green salad, bread sticks, cheese and fruit.*

Overstuffed Chicken

2 cans (10¾ ounces each) condensed golden mushroom soup
⅔ cup water
1 package (8 ounces) herb
  seasoned stuffing
¼ cup melted butter or
  margarine

2 split broilers (about 2½ pounds
  each)
Paprika
⅓ cup chopped onion
Generous dash poultry seasoning
2 tablespoons butter or
  margarine

Combine soup with water. In roasting pan (15½x10½x2¼ inches), mix ⅔ cup soup mixture with stuffing and melted butter. Place broilers over stuffing; sprinkle with paprika. Cover; bake at 400°F. for 1 hour. Uncover; bake 30 minutes longer or until tender. Meanwhile, in saucepan, cook onion with seasoning in butter until tender. Stir in remaining soup mixture. Heat; stir occasionally. Serve with chicken and stuffing. 4 servings.

Cordon Bleu, *using chicken, is an excellent adaptation of the German veal, ham and cheese dish which was awarded the famed French blue ribbon in the late 1700s.*

❈ Cordon Bleu

3 chicken breasts (about
  2½ pounds), split, skinned,
  and boned
3 slices (4 ounces) Swiss cheese,
  cut in half
3 slices (4 ounces) boiled ham,
  cut in half

2 tablespoons butter or
  margarine
1 can (10¾ ounces) condensed
  cream of chicken soup
¼ cup milk or light cream
Chopped parsley

Flatten chicken breasts with flat side of knife. Top each with ½ slice cheese, then ham; secure with toothpicks. In skillet, brown chicken-side down in butter. Stir in soup and milk. Cover; cook over low heat for 20 minutes or until tender. Stir occasionally. Garnish with parsley. 6 servings.

Chicken Stephanie

2 chicken breasts (about 1½
  pounds), split
2 tablespoons shortening
1 can (10¾ ounces) condensed
  cream of chicken soup

¼ cup light cream
¼ cup sherry
1 package (6 ounces) frozen crab,
  thawed and drained

In skillet, brown chicken in shortening; pour off fat. Add remaining ingredients except crab. Cover; cook over low heat 30 minutes or until chicken is tender. Stir occasionally. Add crab; heat. 4 servings.

Swedish Chicken Balls

1 can (10¾ ounces) condensed
  cream of celery soup
1½ cups finely chopped cooked
  chicken or turkey
1 egg, slightly beaten
¼ cup fine dry bread crumbs
¼ teaspoon marjoram, crushed

¼ teaspoon salt
Generous dash pepper
¼ teaspoon chervil, crushed
2 tablespoons butter or
  margarine
⅓ cup milk

Mix *thoroughly* ¼ cup soup, chicken, egg, bread crumbs, marjoram, salt, and pepper. Chill 1 hour. Shape *firmly* into 16 balls. In skillet, brown chicken balls with chervil in butter. Stir in remaining soup and milk. Heat; stir occasionally. Makes about 2 cups.

Arroz con Pollo

2 pounds chicken parts
2 tablespoons salad oil
1 can (10¾ ounces) condensed
  chicken broth
1 can (16 ounces) tomatoes, cut up
⅓ cup water
½ cup chopped onion
2 medium cloves garlic, minced
1 teaspoon salt

¼ teaspoon saffron, crushed, or
  turmeric
⅛ teaspoon pepper
1 medium bay leaf
1 package (10 ounces) frozen
  peas
1 cup raw regular rice
¼ cup sliced stuffed or ripe
  olives

In skillet, brown chicken in oil; pour off fat. Add broth, tomatoes, water, onion, garlic, salt, saffron, pepper, and bay. Cover; cook over low heat 15 minutes. Add remaining ingredients. Cover; cook 30 minutes more or until chicken and rice are tender. Stir occasionally. 4 servings.

❋ Quick Chicken Divan

1 package (10 ounces) frozen
  asparagus or broccoli spears,
  cooked and drained
3 to 4 servings sliced cooked
  chicken or turkey

1 can (10¾ ounces) condensed
  cream of chicken or
  mushroom soup
⅓ cup milk
½ cup shredded Cheddar cheese

Layer asparagus in a shallow baking dish (10x6x2 inches); top with sliced chicken. Blend soup and milk; pour over all; sprinkle with cheese. Broil about 4 to 5 inches from heat until hot and lightly browned on top — about 8 minutes. (Or bake at 450°F. — about 15 minutes.) 3 to 4 servings.

Baked Fondue

4 eggs, separated
1 can (10¾ ounces) condensed
   cream of mushroom soup
2 cups dry bread cubes
1 cup diced cooked chicken or turkey
⅓ cup shredded sharp process cheese

¼ cup toasted slivered almonds
1 tablespoon grated onion
1 tablespoon chopped parsley
⅛ teaspoon marjoram, crushed
⅛ teaspoon thyme, crushed

Beat egg whites until stiff but not dry; beat yolks until thick. Combine yolks, soup, bread, chicken, cheese, almonds, onion, and herbs; gently fold in whites. Pour into 1½-quart casserole. Bake at 325°F. for 1 hour. 4 servings.

❋ 3-Way a la King

2 tablespoons chopped green pepper
¼ cup chopped onion
2 tablespoons butter or margarine
1 can (10¾ ounces) condensed cream
   of chicken or mushroom soup

⅓ to ½ cup milk
1½ cups cubed cooked
   chicken, ham, or turkey
2 tablespoons diced pimiento
Patty shells, toast, or rice

In saucepan, cook green pepper and onion in butter until tender. Blend in soup and milk; add chicken and pimiento. Heat; stir occasionally. Serve in patty shells. Makes about 2½ cups.

Chicken Kiev

½ cup butter or margarine, softened
1 tablespoon chopped parsley
1 medium clove garlic, minced
¼ teaspoon rosemary, crushed
Dash pepper
3 chicken breasts (about 2½
   pounds), split, skinned, and boned
1 egg, slightly beaten

½ cup fine dry bread crumbs
2 tablespoons chopped onion
1 tablespoon chopped parsley
2 tablespoons butter or margarine
1 can (10¾ ounces) condensed
   cream of chicken soup
⅓ cup milk
2 tablespoons sherry or brandy

Blend ½ cup butter, parsley, garlic, rosemary, and pepper. On waxed paper, form butter mixture into patty ¾-inch thick; place in freezer until firm. Meanwhile, flatten chicken breasts with flat side of knife to ¼-inch thickness. Cut butter into 6 equal pieces; place one in center of each breast. Tuck in ends; roll up tightly. Secure with toothpicks. Dip in egg, then in bread crumbs; chill. Fry in deep fat at 350°F. for 10 to 12 minutes or until well browned. Drain on absorbent paper. To make sauce, in saucepan, cook onion with parsley in 2 tablespoons butter until tender. Blend in soup, milk, and sherry. Heat; stir occasionally. Serve with roll-ups. Makes 6 servings.

Brunswick Stew

2 slices bacon
2 pounds chicken parts
1/2 cup sliced onion
1 medium clove garlic, minced
1 can (10¾ ounces) condensed
   tomato soup
1/3 cup water

1 teaspoon Worcestershire
1/4 teaspoon salt
Dash pepper
1 package (10 ounces) frozen
   okra
1 package (10 ounces) frozen
   succotash

In large pan, cook bacon until crisp; remove and crumble. Pour off all but 2 table-spoons drippings. Brown chicken and cook onion with garlic in drippings until tender. Stir in soup, water, Worcestershire, salt, and pepper. Cover; cook over low heat 15 minutes. Add vegetables. Cook 30 minutes more or until tender, stirring vegetables into sauce. Garnish with bacon. 4 servings.

Old Fashioned Chicken and Noodles

1 can (10¾ ounces) condensed
   cream of chicken soup
1/3 cup milk
1/4 teaspoon dry mustard
1/4 teaspoon salt
Generous dash pepper
1½ cups diced cooked chicken

2 cups cooked noodles
1 can (8 ounces) whole
   kernel corn, drained
1/4 cup finely chopped onion
1/4 cup buttered bread crumbs
1 hard-cooked egg, sliced

In 1½-quart casserole, blend soup, milk, mustard, salt, and pepper. Stir in chicken, noodles, corn, and onion. Bake at 400°F. for 25 minutes or until hot; stir. Top with bread crumbs. Bake 5 minutes more. Garnish with egg. Makes about 4½ cups.

Chicken Asparagus Pie

1 can (10¾ ounces) condensed
   cream of celery soup
1 cup cubed cooked chicken
2 hard-cooked eggs, coarsely
   chopped
1 package (10 ounces) frozen
   cut asparagus, cooked and drained

1/3 cup finely chopped celery
2 tablespoons chopped pimiento
1/3 cup sherry
Dash mace
Pastry for 9-inch pie

In 9-inch round shallow baking dish, combine all ingredients except pastry. Roll pastry to fit top of dish. Place on soup mixture; trim edges to fit dish. Make several slits in pastry. Bake at 450°F. for 20 minutes or until done. 4 servings.

The place of origin of Brunswick Stew, *a favorite southern dish, is disputed. It is claimed by Brunswick County, Georgia; Brunswick County, Virginia; and Brunswick County, North Carolina.*

Livers Paprikash

2 packages (8 ounces each)
  frozen chicken livers
2 tablespoons butter or
  margarine
1/2 cup chopped celery
1/4 cup chopped onion

1 can (10¾ ounces) condensed
  cream of mushroom soup
1/2 cup milk or sour cream
1/2 teaspoon paprika
Cooked noodles or toast

In covered skillet, cook chicken livers in butter over low heat until completely thawed (about 15 minutes). Stir occasionally. Uncover; lightly brown livers and cook celery and onion until tender. Blend in soup, milk, and paprika. Heat; stir occasionally. Serve over noodles. Makes about 3 cups.

Hot Club Sandwich

4 servings sliced cooked chicken
8 slices cooked bacon
4 tomato slices
4 slices toast

1 can (11 ounces) condensed
  Cheddar cheese soup
1/2 cup sour cream

Arrange chicken, bacon, and tomato on each slice of toast. In saucepan, blend soup and sour cream. Heat; stir occasionally. Pour over sandwiches. Makes 4 open-face sandwiches.

Duckling Montmorency

1 duckling (about 5 pounds)
1/2 teaspoon salt
1/8 teaspoon pepper
Dash ground thyme
1 can (16 ounces) pitted dark
  sweet cherries

1/2 to ¾ cup Port or other sweet
  red wine
1 can (10½ ounces) condensed
  beef broth
1 tablespoon lemon juice
1 tablespoon cornstarch

Season cavity of duckling with salt, pepper, and thyme. Prick skin and place breast-side up on rack in shallow baking pan. Roast at 325°F. for about 3 hours (30 to 35 minutes per pound or until tender). Meanwhile, drain cherries, reserving 1/4 cup of the liquid. Let cherries stand in Port. Drain juices from cavity and remove duckling to serving platter; keep warm. Skim fat from drippings; add Port drained from cherries. Bring to boil; stir to loosen browned bits. Add broth, cherries, and lemon juice. Blend cornstarch into reserved cherry liquid; add to roasting pan. Cook, stirring constantly until thickened and clear. Spoon some sauce over duckling; serve with remaining sauce. 4 servings.

Regal fare that features a wine-flavored cherry sauce: Duckling Montmorency.

CHEESE
EGGS · PASTA

These three favorite foods have an affinity for each other and combine harmoniously in delightful culinary creations. They also have great appeal when cooked separately or with other enticing fare.

We relish cheese, by itself, as snack, appetizer and dessert. Very popular, too, are soups, sauces, souffles, casseroles and pasta creations made with cheeses. In recent years Switzerland's fondue has proved an intriguing addition to the list.

A good selection of cheeses, both domestic and imported, is now available. Fortunately, many of them are interchangeable in recipes. We have become well acquainted with the qualities and uses of the basic types, such as cottage or Cheddar, as well as more exotic ones like ricotta, Muenster, and Camembert.

If any food is all-important to cookery, it must be the egg. By itself, it is nutritious and appealing. And it is significant in many other roles in cookery — thickening sauces, binding ingredients, garnishing foods. Eggs are served for every meal and have a place in every course. Poached, fried, baked, scrambled, hard-cooked or made into omelets, they combine with other foods to make attractive party dishes. Eggs are elementary, economical but also exceptional and elegant.

The preparation of pasta has become extremely popular in America in recent years. Fortunately a galaxy of fascinating pasta products — lasagna, manicotti, spaghetti, macaroni and vermicelli — is readily available in our stores. Pasta dishes are valued for entertaining as they can be prepared ahead of time and are most attractive served in casseroles for buffets or informal dining.

Saucy Baked Eggs

1 can (10¾ ounces) condensed
    cream of chicken soup
⅓ cup light cream
½ cup shredded natural Swiss
    cheese

2 tablespoons grated Parmesan
    cheese
10 eggs

In saucepan, combine all ingredients except eggs. Heat until cheese melts; stir occasionally. For each serving, break two eggs into individual baking dishes or custard cups (6-ounce size); cover with sauce. Sprinkle with additional Parmesan cheese. Bake at 350°F. for 10 to 15 minutes until eggs are desired doneness. 5 servings.

Huevos Rancheros

¼ cup chopped onion
2 to 3 teaspoons chili powder
1 large clove garlic, minced
2 tablespoons butter or
    margarine

1 can (10¾ ounces) condensed
    tomato soup
½ cup water
6 eggs
6 slices toast or tortillas

In skillet, cook onion with chili and garlic in butter until tender. Add soup and water; bring to boil. Gently slip eggs into soup sauce. Cover; cook over low heat until whites are firm. Serve eggs on toast with sauce. 6 servings.

❋ Easy Souffle

1 can (10¾ ounces) condensed
    cream of celery, chicken, or
    mushroom soup
1 cup shredded sharp process
    cheese

2 to 3 teaspoons curry powder,
    optional
6 eggs, separated

In saucepan, combine soup and cheese; add curry powder if desired. Heat slowly until cheese melts. Stir occasionally. Remove from heat. Beat egg yolks until thick and lemon colored; gradually stir in soup mixture. In large bowl, beat egg whites until stiff; fold soup mixture into egg whites. Pour into ungreased 2-quart casserole. Bake at 300°F. about 1 to 1¼ hours or until souffle is brown. Serve immediately. 4 to 6 servings.

Puffy Omelet with Avocado Sauce

Omelet:

6 eggs, separated	Dash pepper
1/3 cup milk	3 tablespoons butter
1/4 teaspoon salt	or margarine

Beat egg whites until stiff. Beat yolks until thick and lemon colored; beat in milk, salt, and pepper; fold into whites. Heat butter in oven-proof skillet; pour in eggs. Cook over low heat about 5 minutes or until lightly browned on bottom. Bake at 350°F. for 10 to 15 minutes or until top springs back when pressed with finger.

Sauce:

1/4 cup sliced green onions	1/3 cup milk
1 teaspoon curry powder	1 teaspoon lemon juice
1 tablespoon butter or margarine	1 small avocado, peeled and
1 can (10¾ ounces) condensed	cubed
cream of mushroom soup	

Meanwhile, in saucepan, cook onions with curry in butter until tender. Add soup, milk, and lemon juice. Heat; stir occasionally. Add avocado just before serving. When omelet is done, transfer to platter. Make a shallow cut down the center; pour part of sauce on; fold in half. Top with remaining sauce. 4 servings.

❋ Crispy Macaroni and Cheese

1 can (10¾ ounces) condensed	Generous dash pepper
cream of celery or mushroom soup	3 cups cooked elbow macaroni
1/2 cup milk	2 cups shredded Cheddar cheese
1/2 teaspoon prepared mustard	1 can (3½ ounces) French
	fried onions

In 1½-quart casserole, blend soup, milk, mustard, and pepper. Stir in macaroni and 1½ cups cheese. Bake at 400°F. for 25 minutes or until hot; stir. Top with onions and remaining cheese; bake 5 minutes more. Makes about 4½ cups.

❋ Spaghetti with White Clam Sauce

1 can (7½ ounces) minced clams	1/4 cup milk or light cream
2 medium cloves garlic, minced	1 to 2 tablespoons grated
2 tablespoons chopped parsley	Parmesan cheese
2 tablespoons butter or margarine	Cooked spaghetti
1 can (10¾ ounces) condensed	
cream of mushroom soup	

Drain clams; reserve liquid. In saucepan, cook clams, garlic, and parsley in butter a few minutes. Stir in soup, milk, clam liquid, and cheese. Cook over low heat 10 minutes. Stir occasionally. Serve over spaghetti. Makes about 2 cups.

✳ *Spaghetti with Meat Sauce*

1 pound ground beef
1 cup chopped onion
1 teaspoon basil, crushed
2 teaspoons oregano, crushed
2 large cloves garlic, minced

2 cans (10¾ ounces each)
    condensed tomato soup
1 can (16 ounces) tomatoes
½ pound spaghetti, cooked and
    drained
Grated Parmesan cheese

In saucepan, brown beef and cook onion with seasonings until onion is tender. Add soup and tomatoes. Stir to break up tomatoes. Cook over low heat 30 minutes; stir occasionally. Serve over spaghetti with Parmesan. Makes about 4½ cups.

✳ *Lasagna*

½ pound ground beef
1 cup chopped onion
2 large cloves garlic, minced
2 teaspoons oregano, crushed
2 cans (10¾ ounces each)
    condensed tomato soup
½ cup water
2 teaspoons vinegar

9 lasagna noodles (about
    ½ pound), cooked and
    drained
1 pint small or large curd
    cottage cheese or ricotta cheese
1½ cups shredded Mozzarella cheese
Grated Parmesan cheese

Available to today's cook are over 100 pasta products. Get to know a variety of them to make memorable and rewarding fare.

In saucepan, brown beef and cook onion, garlic, and oregano until onion is tender. Add soup, water, and vinegar. Cook over low heat 30 minutes; stir occasionally. In shallow baking dish (12x8x2 inches), arrange 3 alternate layers of noodles, cottage cheese, meat sauce, and Mozzarella cheese. Sprinkle with Parmesan cheese. Bake at 350°F. for 30 minutes. Let stand 15 minutes before serving. 6 servings.

✳ *Parmesan Noodles*

1 can (10¾ ounces) condensed
    cream of mushroom or
    tomato soup *
¾ cup milk

½ cup grated Parmesan cheese
3 cups hot cooked noodles
4 tablespoons butter
    or margarine

In large saucepan, stir soup until smooth; blend in milk and cheese. Heat; stir occasionally. *Just before serving,* toss *hot* noodles with butter; combine with soup mixture. Serve with additional cheese. Makes about 3½ cups.

*When using tomato soup substitute light cream for milk.

Bring a little of the magic of Rome to your table with any one of these pasta specialties: Parmesan Noodles, Spaghetti *and* Lasagna.

VEGETABLES

Seek variety when you select and cook vegetables. Despite the diverse types of these delicious and colorful foods, we too often offer the same familiar vegetables prepared in the simplest manner. We tend to take them for granted and fail to treat them with imagination.

The art of vegetable cookery is one of the easiest to master. Vegetables, whether frozen, canned or fresh, should be cooked until just tender. For a change from the usual, serve braised, baked or stuffed vegetables to enhance a meal. Prepared as souffles or cooked with piquant sauces, vegetables may become a specialty of the house. Herbs and seasonings give new dimensions even to ordinary carrots, spinach or peas.

Over the centuries the social status of vegetables has changed and fluctuated remarkably. Mushrooms were not really accepted here as a culinary marvel until recent years. The potato was shunned in both the Old and New World, from whence it came, until its beneficial qualities as a food were finally realized, only in the early 1700s. Two "relatives," the eggplant and tomato, dubbed the "mad apple" and "love apple," were long suspected to be poisonous and even in colonial America were grown as curiosities.

All vegetables are worthy of interest. Attractive to serve, they may be delectable appetizers, first courses, side dishes or main dishes for luncheons and suppers. Remember too, that they add particular sparkle and color to a buffet or dinner table.

In vegetable cookery there is great opportunity for imaginative preparation and serving to lift these foods out of the background and make them a special attraction both for everyday and company meals.

Stuffed Zucchini

6 small zucchini (about 2 pounds)
½ pound ground beef
⅓ cup chopped onion
1 large clove garlic, minced
1 teaspoon oregano, crushed

2 tablespoons olive oil
1 can (11 ounces) condensed
   tomato bisque soup
¼ cup grated Parmesan cheese

Cut lengthwise slice from top of zucchini; scoop out seeds and pulp leaving ¼-inch shell. Coarsely chop pulp and seeds. In skillet, brown beef and cook onion, garlic, and oregano in oil until onion is tender. Add zucchini pulp and seeds, ¼ cup soup, and Parmesan. Spoon into zucchini shells; arrange in shallow baking dish (12x8x2 inches). Pour remaining soup over and around stuffed zucchini; sprinkle with additional Parmesan. Cover; bake at 375°F. for 40 minutes or until tender. Uncover; bake 5 minutes more. 6 servings.

Holiday Carrots and Onions

1 pound (about 8) carrots,
   halved lengthwise
1 pound (about 18) small
   whole white onions

1 can (10¾ ounces) condensed
   cream of mushroom soup
1 tablespoon chopped parsley
¼ teaspoon paprika
Toasted slivered almonds

The carrot, a very ancient vegetable, rates today as a staple in almost every kitchen. Eaten both in its delightfully crisp raw state as well as cooked, it also wins praise for its rich hue (orange is sometimes described as the most "edible" color).

Cut carrots in 3-inch pieces. In covered saucepan, cook carrots and onions in water for 30 minutes or until tender. Drain. Stir in soup, ½ cup water, parsley, and paprika. Heat; stir occasionally. Garnish with almonds. Makes about 4 cups.

Honey Glazed Sweet Potatoes

1 can (10½ ounces) condensed
   consomme
¼ cup honey
1 tablespoon cornstarch
1 teaspoon grated orange rind

Generous dash cinnamon
4 medium sweet potatoes
   (about 2 pounds), cooked,
   peeled, and cut in half

In skillet, combine all ingredients except potatoes. Cook, stirring until thickened. Add potatoes. Cook over low heat 10 minutes or until potatoes are glazed, basting frequently. 4 to 6 servings.

Capture the accolades of your guests by surprising them with different vegetable creations. This trio: Stuffed Zucchini, Holiday Carrots and Onions and Honey Glazed Sweet Potatoes.

❈ Easy Creamed Vegetables

2 packages (9 to 10 ounces
  each) frozen cauliflower,
  corn, green beans, lima beans,
  mixed vegetables, peas, peas
  and carrots, carrots,

or spinach
1 can (10¾ ounces) condensed
  cream of celery, chicken,
  or mushroom soup

Cook vegetables in unsalted water until tender; drain. Stir in soup. Heat; stir occasionally. Thin to desired consistency with milk. Makes about 4 cups.

❈ Green Bean Bake

1 can (10¾ ounces) condensed
  cream of mushroom soup
½ cup milk
1 teaspoon soy sauce
Dash pepper

2 packages (9 ounces each)
  frozen green beans, cooked
  and drained
1 can (3½ ounces) French
  fried onions

In 1½-quart casserole, stir soup, milk, soy, and pepper until smooth; mix in green beans and ½ can onions. Bake at 350°F. for 25 minutes; stir. Top with remaining onions. Bake 5 minutes more. Makes about 4 cups.

Ratatouille

3 small zucchini, sliced (3 cups)
2 medium green peppers, cut
  into strips
1 cup sliced onion
1 large clove garlic, minced
½ teaspoon basil, crushed

2 tablespoons olive oil
1 can (10¾ ounces)
  condensed tomato soup
1 medium eggplant, peeled and
  cubed
½ teaspoon salt

In skillet, cook zucchini, green pepper, onion, garlic, and basil in oil 5 minutes. Add remaining ingredients. Cover; cook over low heat 25 minutes. Stir occasionally. Uncover; cook 5 minutes more. Makes about 6 cups.

Potato Pancakes

1 can (10¾ ounces) condensed
  cream of potato soup
⅓ cup flour
3 eggs

2 tablespoons bacon drippings
½ cup canned corn
2 slices bacon, cooked and
  crumbled
Applesauce or maple syrup

In bowl, blend soup and flour; beat in eggs and drippings. Add corn and bacon. Pour ¼ cup batter for each pancake on hot, lightly greased griddle. Cook until golden brown on each side; turn only once. Serve with applesauce or syrup. Makes 10 pancakes.

Stuffed Acorn Squash

3 acorn squash
Butter
Salt and pepper
¾ pound ground beef
¼ pound bulk sausage

½ cup chopped celery
⅓ cup chopped onion
1 can (10¾ ounces) condensed
  cream of mushroom soup
Buttered bread crumbs

Split squash; remove seeds and fibers. Brush inside and edge with butter; sprinkle with salt and pepper. Bake cut side down in shallow baking dish at 400°F. for 35 minutes. Meanwhile, in skillet, cook beef, sausage, celery, and onion until meat is browned and celery is tender. Stir in soup. Fill squash with mixture; top with crumbs. Bake 20 minutes more or until tender. 6 servings.

Chinese Vegetables

2 cups diagonally sliced celery
1 cup diagonally sliced green
  onion
2 tablespoons salad oil
1 can (10¾ ounces) condensed
  chicken broth
1 can (16 ounces) bean sprouts,
  drained

⅓ cup bamboo shoots
⅓ cup sliced water chestnuts
2 tablespoons cornstarch
2 tablespoons soy sauce
Cooked rice

In skillet, cook celery and onion in oil until just tender. Add remaining ingredients except rice. Cook over low heat, stirring until thickened. Serve over rice with additional soy sauce. Makes about 3½ cups.

The Chinese regard vegetables with high esteem and have perfected the art of cooking them. By using their quick-fry method, vegetables remain crisp, keep their original color and retain valuable nutrients.

Onions with Sausage Stuffing

4 large onions (about 2 pounds),
  peeled
¼ pound bulk sausage
½ teaspoon herb seasoning
1 can (10¾ ounces) condensed
  cream of mushroom soup

¼ cup bread crumbs
½ cup milk
⅛ teaspoon marjoram,
  crushed

In saucepan, cook onions in boiling water 15 minutes; drain. Cut tops off onions; scoop out centers leaving ¼-inch thick shell. Chop onion centers. In skillet, cook sausage with chopped onion and herb seasoning until done; mix in ¼ cup soup and crumbs. Firmly fill onion shells with sausage mixture; arrange in 9-inch pie dish. Add water to just cover bottom of dish. Bake at 350°F. for 40 minutes. Meanwhile in saucepan, combine remaining soup, milk, and marjoram; heat. Serve over onions. 4 servings.

Vegetables a la Grecque

Despite the name this colorful vegetable medley is a most popular hors d'oeuvre in lovely French Provence along the Mediterranean. It is also a marvelous accompaniment to meat, poultry or game.

Vegetables:
- 2 cups water
- 9 small whole white onions (½ pound)
- 2 cups whole green beans (¼ pound)
- 2½ cups cauliflowerets (½ pound)
- 2 cups celery strips (¼ pound)
- 1 package (9 ounces) frozen artichokes
- 2 cups small fresh mushroom caps (about ¼ pound)

Marinade:
- 1 can (10¾ ounces) condensed chicken broth
- ½ soup can water
- ⅓ cup lemon juice
- ¼ cup olive oil
- 3 large cloves garlic, minced
- 2 large bay leaves
- 1 teaspoon fennel seed
- 12 peppercorns
- ½ teaspoon ground coriander
- ½ teaspoon ground thyme

In large saucepan, bring water to boil; add onions and beans. Cover; cook over low heat 10 minutes. Add cauliflower and celery; cook 5 minutes more. Add artichokes; cook 5 minutes more. Add mushrooms; cook 5 minutes or until vegetables are just tender; drain. Combine ingredients for marinade; add to vegetables. Cover; bring to boil. Chill; stir occasionally. Arrange drained vegetables on platter; moisten with a few spoonfuls of marinade. Makes about 6 cups.

Baked Stuffed Tomatoes

- 6 medium tomatoes
- 2 slices bacon
- ¼ cup chopped green pepper
- ¼ cup chopped onion
- 1 cup cooked corn
- Generous dash pepper
- ¾ cup toasted buttered bread cubes
- 1 can (10¾ ounces) condensed cream of celery soup
- ¼ cup milk

Cut slice from top of tomatoes; scoop out and save pulp leaving ¼-inch shell. In skillet, cook bacon; remove and crumble. Cook green pepper and onion in drippings until tender; stir in corn, pepper, and all but ½ cup tomato pulp. Cook over low heat 5 minutes. Place 1 tablespoon bread in each tomato; fill with vegetable mixture. Top with remaining bread. Place in baking dish; add water to just cover bottom of dish. Bake at 350°F. for 20 minutes. Meanwhile in saucepan, combine soup, reserved tomato pulp, milk, and bacon; heat but do not boil. Serve over tomatoes. 6 servings.

❊ *Broccoli au Gratin*

1 bunch broccoli (about 2
   pounds) or 1 small head
   cauliflower (or two 10-ounce
   frozen packages of either
   vegetable)
1 can (11 ounces) condensed
   Cheddar cheese soup

1/4 cup milk
2 tablespoons buttered bread
   crumbs
4 slices bacon, cooked and
   crumbled

Cook vegetable; drain. Place in shallow baking dish (10x6x2 inches). Stir soup; blend in milk; pour over vegetable. Top with crumbs. Bake at 350°F. for 20 minutes or until hot. Garnish with bacon before serving. 4 to 6 servings.

Minted Creamed Peas and Celery

2 cups thinly sliced celery
1/4 teaspoon salt
1 cup water
1 package (10 ounces) frozen
   peas

1 can (10¾ ounces) condensed
   cream of chicken soup
1/3 cup milk
1 teaspoon lemon juice
1/4 teaspoon dried mint flakes,
   crushed

In saucepan, combine celery, salt, and water. Cook for 15 minutes or until just tender. Add peas; bring to boil. Cover; cook over low heat 5 minutes or until tender. Drain; add remaining ingredients. Heat; stir occasionally. Makes about 3 cups.

Sweet Sour Cabbage

2 slices bacon
1/2 cup chopped onion
1 can (10¾ ounces) condensed
   chicken broth
1/3 cup wine vinegar
2 tablespoons sugar
Generous dash pepper

3 cups thinly sliced tart
   apples (2 medium)
1 medium bay leaf
7 cups shredded red cabbage,
   1 small head (about 1½
   pounds)
1 tablespoon cornstarch
2 tablespoons water

In skillet, cook bacon; remove and crumble. Cook onion in drippings until tender. Stir in broth, vinegar, sugar, and pepper; add apple and bay. Bring to boil; add cabbage. Cover; cook over medium heat 45 minutes or until tender. Combine cornstarch and water; stir into cabbage. Cook, stirring until slightly thickened. Remove bay leaf. Garnish with bacon. Makes about 4 cups.

In northern and central Europe this is one of the most prized vegetable dishes. It is excellent with pork, game or goose, and is a traditional Christmas dish in many countries.

SALADS and DRESSINGS

"**A** fool can pick a sallet as well as a wise man," goes an old saying. But which salad to choose is another matter, since tastes in salads differ so widely. Fortunately, the variety available permits a selection agreeable to everyone.

In ancient days salads were simply made with edible greens or herbs over which oil, vinegar and spices were poured. The word salad comes from the Latin "sal" or salt, which the Romans commonly used as a food preservative. In Europe salads did not really become fashionable or popular until the 1700s when court cooks, who set the culinary styles, combined numerous ingredients to make them. The vogue in England was to include several kinds of flower petals. "They say primroses make a capital salad," wrote Disraeli.

Today we Americans have become enamored of salads and they now appear in infinite variety. Although generally served cold, some are offered hot. They may be appetizers, first courses, main or side dishes.

World-wide tastes for salads vary greatly. In the Orient they are customarily pickled foods. The French serve salads as appetizers or as a separate course after the entree. A favorite in Germany is made with sauerkraut. In the Middle East they are most often fresh vegetables flavored with oil and lemon juice. South of the border many salads are based on avocados. A salad cart with a display of many varieties in European restaurants is a delight to behold.

In America we have embraced salads from around the world and contributed molded salads made with gelatine, as well as those utilizing fruit, cheeses, and sometimes nuts and raisins. Very important to salads are the many dressings, which can be purchased or homemade.

Chef's Salad with Blue Cheese-Mushroom Dressing

1 medium head lettuce, torn in
  pieces
1 package (10 ounces) frozen
  asparagus spears, cooked,
  drained, and chilled
1 cup cooked chicken cut in strips
1 cup cooked ham cut in strips
2 hard-cooked eggs, sliced

1 can (10¾ ounces) condensed
  cream of mushroom or
  celery soup
½ cup sour cream
¼ cup crumbled blue cheese
2 tablespoons milk
1 tablespoon lemon juice

Place lettuce in salad bowl. Top with an arrangement of asparagus, chicken, ham, and eggs. For dressing, combine remaining ingredients and stir until smooth. Thin to desired consistency with additional milk. Chill. Serve with salad. 4 servings.

Serve sparkling salad . . . either Ribbon Aspic *or* Chef's *as the main course for a special luncheon.*

Ribbon Aspic

Cheese Layer:
- 1 envelope unflavored gelatine
- ½ cup milk
- 3 cups small curd cottage cheese
- ½ cup chopped cucumber
- 2 tablespoons finely chopped onion

Aspic Layer:
- 1 envelope unflavored gelatine
- ½ cup cold water
- 1 can (10¾ ounces) condensed tomato soup
- 1 tablespoon lemon juice
- ½ teaspoon dried dill weed, crushed
- 1½ cups diced cooked shrimp

In saucepan, sprinkle 1 envelope gelatine on milk to soften. Place over low heat, stirring until gelatine is dissolved. Remove from heat; stir in cheese, cucumber, and onion. In bottom of loaf pan (9x5x3 inches), spoon in half of cheese mixture. Chill until slightly firm. Meanwhile, in saucepan, sprinkle 1 envelope gelatine on ½ cup cold water to soften. Place over low heat, stirring until gelatine is dissolved. Remove from heat; stir in soup, juice, and dill. Chill until slightly thickened. Fold in shrimp. Pour onto cheese layer. Chill until slightly firm. Top with remaining cheese mixture. Chill until firm. Unmold; garnish with shrimp, cucumber, and pimiento strips if desired. 6 to 8 servings.

❋ Potato-Ham Salad

1 can (10¾ ounces) condensed
   cream of celery soup
¼ cup water
2 teaspoons vinegar
⅛ teaspoon pepper
3 cups cubed cooked potatoes

1½ cups cubed cooked ham
¼ cup diced sweet pickle
2 tablespoons finely chopped
   green onions
Sliced hard-cooked egg
Parsley sprigs

In large bowl, blend soup, water, vinegar, and pepper. Add potatoes, ham, pickle, and onion. Chill. Garnish with egg and parsley. Makes about 5 cups.
To serve hot: Increase water to ½ cup. In skillet, prepare as above. Heat; stir occasionally.

Cucumbers in Sour Cream Dressing

1 can (10¾ ounces) condensed
   cream of celery soup
½ cup sour cream
2 tablespoons finely chopped dill
   pickle
2 tablespoons finely chopped
   onion

2 tablespoons finely chopped
   radishes
Generous dash pepper
4 cups thinly sliced cucumbers
   (about 4 medium cucumbers)
Lettuce
Parsley

Mix soup, sour cream, pickle, onion, radish, and pepper; add cucumbers. Chill. Serve on lettuce; garnish with parsley and additional radishes. Makes about 4 cups.

Remoulade Dressing

1 can (10¾ ounces) condensed
   cream of celery soup
⅓ cup mayonnaise
¼ cup chopped sweet pickle
1 tablespoon capers, drained

1 tablespoon chopped anchovies
1 tablespoon chopped parsley
¼ teaspoon dry mustard
Generous dash crushed tarragon

Thoroughly mix all ingredients. Chill. Thin with additional milk if desired. Serve with cold sliced chicken or flaked crab meat on salad greens. Makes about 2 cups.

Molded Borsch

1 envelope unflavored gelatine
¾ cup cold water
1 can (10½ ounces) condensed
   consomme

1 can (8 ounces) diced beets
1 tablespoon lemon juice
2 tablespoons thinly sliced green
   onion
1 cup sour cream

In saucepan, sprinkle gelatine on cold water to soften. Place over low heat, stirring until gelatine is dissolved. Remove from heat; stir in consomme, liquid from beets, and lemon juice. Chill until slightly thickened. Fold in beets and 1 tablespoon onion. Pour into 4-cup ring mold and chill until firm. Unmold on lettuce. Fill center of mold with sour cream; garnish with remaining onion. Makes about 4 cups.

Molded Borsch *translates the beloved Polish and Russian soup into sparkling ruby salad. Bright to see and taste.*

Tomatoes with Shrimp Stuffing

1 can (10¾ ounces) condensed
   cream of asparagus soup
½ cup sour cream
1 teaspoon lemon juice
¼ teaspoon Worcestershire
⅛ teaspoon dried dill weed

2 cups diced cooked shrimp
½ cup diced cucumber
¼ cup chopped green pepper
4 medium tomatoes
Salad greens

In bowl, blend soup, sour cream, lemon juice, Worcestershire, and dill. Add shrimp, cucumber, and green pepper; chill. Place tomatoes stem end down. With knife, cut each tomato almost to stem end, making 5 or 6 sections; spread apart slightly. Place on greens; fill between slices with shrimp mixture. 4 servings.

❊ Tomato French Dressing
Pictured on back cover

1 can (10¾ ounces) condensed
   tomato soup
½ cup salad oil

¼ cup vinegar
½ teaspoon dry mustard

Combine ingredients in a jar; shake well before using. (Or mix in an electric blender.) Makes about 1½ cups. Serve with salad greens.

Variations: To 1 recipe of Tomato French Dressing add any one of the following:
- 4 slices bacon, cooked and crumbled
- ¼ cup crumbled blue cheese
- 1 medium clove garlic, minced
- ¼ cup sweet pickle relish

BARBECUES

One of the most popular forms of entertaining is the barbecue. It presents the hostess with an opportunity to create an informal and attractive occasion with a minimum of effort. Whether enjoyed indoors or out, much of the preparation can be done beforehand, and it is not unusual for the host to participate in the culinary chores.

It was probably in pre-historic times that man discovered, doubtlessly by accident, the miracles that fire worked upon his food. Later, roaming herdsmen found that tough mutton, cut into small pieces, marinated and cooked on sticks over low fires, tasted much better than before. Archaeological finds in the Middle East testify that as early as 3000 B.C. man was utilizing movable metal hearths, metal spits and other gadgetry to enhance preparation of his food.

In medieval Europe whole carcasses of animals were cooked on spits, often in the dining hall fireplace. Our colonial forefathers used large kitchen fireplaces or outside shelters for this type of cookery.

Over the decades American cooks have devised fascinating recipes for favorite meats, poultry and seafood in barbecue sauces. The popularity of outdoor cookery on grills, hibachis, or over open fires has reached new peaks. Many of the same or different dishes can be prepared in our excellent indoor ovens or electric rotisseries, and enjoyed in the dining room, or brought to the patio, porch or backyard.

We are all fond of these appealing foods in their savory combinations. Excellent for family get-togethers and entertaining friends, the barbecue lets everyone enjoy the tantalizing aromas of the actual cookery, and then the irresistible results.

Barbecuing goes with dining al fresco which leads to some of life's most memorable meals — whether on the beach at sunset, in an autumn woods, or just your own backyard.

❋ *All 'Round Barbecue Sauce*

1 can (10¾ ounces) condensed tomato soup	¼ cup chopped onion
2 to 4 tablespoons sweet pickle relish	1 tablespoon brown sugar
	1 tablespoon vinegar
	1 tablespoon Worcestershire

In saucepan, combine all ingredients. Cover; cook over low heat 10 minutes. Stir occasionally. Makes 1½ cups sauce.

❋ *Zippy Barbecue Sauce*

⅓ cup chopped onion	2 tablespoons brown sugar
1 small clove garlic, minced	1 tablespoon vinegar
2 tablespoons salad oil	1 to 2 tablespoons Worcestershire
1 can (10¾ ounces) condensed tomato soup	1 teaspoon prepared mustard
	Dash hot pepper sauce

In saucepan, cook onion and garlic in oil until tender; add remaining ingredients. Cook over low heat 15 minutes; stir occasionally. Makes 1½ cups sauce.
Note: Use either of the above sauces with the meats listed below. Guaranteed successful barbecuing!

Indoor Method:

Chicken: Brush 2 split broilers (2½ pounds each) with salad oil; place on broiler pan, skin-side down, 6 inches from heat.* Cook 15 minutes on each side. Brush with sauce; cook 30 minutes more or until chicken is tender, turning and brushing with sauce every 5 minutes. 4 servings.
*For gas broiler, follow manufacturer's directions.

Frankfurter: Slit 1 pound frankfurters. Broil 4 inches from heat for 10 minutes, turning and brushing with sauce. Serve on toasted frankfurter buns with remaining sauce. 4 to 5 servings.

Hamburger: Season 2 pounds ground beef with 1 teaspoon salt and dash pepper; shape into 8 patties. Broil 4 inches from heat for 15 minutes or until desired doneness, turning and brushing with sauce every 5 minutes. Serve on toasted hamburger buns with remaining sauce. 8 servings.

Sparerib: In large heavy pan, cover 4 pounds spareribs, cut in serving-size pieces, with water. Simmer 1 hour; drain. Place ribs on broiler pan. Broil 6 inches from heat* for 30 minutes, turning and brushing with sauce every 5 minutes. 4 servings.
*For gas broiler, follow manufacturer's directions.

Steak: Place 2-pound sirloin steak (about 1-inch thick) on broiler pan; brush with sauce. Broil 4 inches from heat for 4 to 5 minutes. Turn; brush with sauce. Broil 4 minutes more or until desired doneness. Heat remaining sauce; serve with steak. 4 to 6 servings.

Outdoor Method:

Chicken: Brush 2 split broilers (2½ pounds each) with salad oil; place on grill, skin-side up, about 6 inches above single layer of glowing coals. Cook 15 minutes on each side. Brush with sauce; cook 30 minutes more or until chicken is tender, turning and brushing with sauce every 5 minutes. 4 servings.

Frankfurter: Slit 1 pound frankfurters. Place on grill 4 inches above glowing coals. Cook, turning and brushing with sauce until browned. Heat remaining sauce; serve with frankfurters. 4 to 5 servings.

Hamburger: To prepare hamburgers, see Indoor Method. Place hamburgers on grill 4 inches above glowing coals. Cook 5 minutes brushing with sauce. Turn; continue brushing with sauce. Cook 5 minutes more or until desired doneness. 8 servings.

Sparerib: Precook spareribs following Indoor Method. Place spareribs on grill 6 inches above glowing coals. Cook 30 minutes, turning and brushing with sauce every 5 minutes. 4 servings.

Steak: Place 2-pound sirloin steak (about 1-inch thick) on grill 4 inches above glowing coals. Cook 5 minutes, brushing with sauce. Turn; continue brushing with sauce. Cook 5 minutes more or until desired doneness. Heat remaining sauce; serve with steak. 4 to 6 servings.

Chicken-Shrimp Kabobs, Curry Sauce

¼ cup chopped onion
1 tablespoon curry powder
2 tablespoons butter or margarine
1 can (10¾ ounces) condensed
   chicken broth

4 teaspoons cornstarch
½ cup currant jelly
1 tablespoon lime juice

In saucepan, cook onion with curry in butter until tender. Remove from heat. Add remaining ingredients. Cook over low heat, stirring until thickened. Serve as barbecue sauce for Chicken-Shrimp Kabobs.

Chicken-Shrimp Kabobs: Prepare sauce. On 4 skewers arrange alternately: 1 chicken breast (about 1 pound), split, skinned, and boned, cut into 8 strips; 8 large raw shrimp (about ½ pound), cleaned; 8 green pepper squares (1 inch); 8 cherry tomatoes. 4 servings.

Indoor Method: Broil about 4 inches from heat 15 minutes or until done, turning and brushing with sauce every 5 minutes. Heat remaining sauce; serve with kabobs.

Outdoor Method: Brush kabobs lightly with salad oil. Place on grill 4 inches above glowing coals; cook 15 minutes or until done, turning and brushing with sauce every 5 minutes. Heat remaining sauce; serve with kabobs.

Company Chicken Cook-out

1 can (10¾ ounces) condensed
    cream of mushroom soup
1 can (10½ ounces) condensed
    onion soup
½ cup ketchup
¼ cup salad oil

¼ cup vinegar
2 large cloves garlic, minced
2 tablespoons brown sugar
1 tablespoon Worcestershire
⅛ teaspoon hot pepper sauce
4 split broilers (2½ pounds each)

In saucepan, combine all ingredients except chicken. Cover; cook over low heat about 15 minutes. Stir occasionally. Brush split broilers with salad oil; place on grill, skin-side up, about 6 inches above single layer of glowing coals. Cook 15 minutes on each side. Brush with sauce; cook 30 minutes more or until chicken is tender, turning and brushing with sauce every 5 minutes. 8 servings.

❈ Ribs with Apricot Barbecue Sauce

½ cup chopped onion
1 large clove garlic, minced
2 tablespoons salad oil
1 can (10½ ounces) condensed
    beef broth

1 cup apricot preserves
    (12-ounce jar)
¼ cup lemon juice
4 teaspoons soy sauce

In saucepan, cook onion and garlic in oil until onion is tender. Add remaining ingredients. Cover; cook over low heat 15 minutes. Stir occasionally. Makes about 2 cups sauce. Serve as barbecue sauce for spareribs, following Indoor Method p. 112. Reduce broiling time to 20 minutes.

Brush grill with oil before cooking. Meat should be at room temperature. Use marinades to flavor and tenderize less expensive cuts of meats and poultry. Keep the fare simple but good. Create an informal but attractive setting.

Lamb Chops Polynesian

1 can (10½ ounces) condensed
    onion soup
¼ cup drained crushed pineapple
2 tablespoons brown sugar
1 teaspoon cornstarch
⅛ teaspoon ground allspice

⅛ teaspoon ground coriander
8 lamb or veal chops, 1-inch
    thick (about 2 to 2½
    pounds)
Salad oil

In saucepan, combine soup, pineapple, brown sugar, cornstarch, allspice, and coriander. Cook, stirring until thickened. Brush chops lightly with oil. Place on grill 4 inches above glowing coals. Cook for 10 minutes, brushing with sauce. Turn; continue brushing with sauce. Cook 10 minutes more or until desired doneness. Heat remaining sauce; serve with chops. 4 servings.

*Zippy Barbecue Sauce tops Chicken on the grill . . .
to be served with roasting ears for a picnic to please!*

Tony's Barbecued Burgers

1 can (10¾ ounces) condensed
tomato soup
1 can (2 ounces) mushrooms,
drained and chopped

¼ cup chopped onion
1 small clove garlic, minced
1 teaspoon oregano, crushed

In saucepan, combine all ingredients. Cover; cook over low heat 10 minutes. Stir occasionally. Thin with water, if desired. Makes about 1½ cups sauce. Serve as barbecue sauce for hamburgers, following Indoor Method p. 112.

Saucy Beef Kabobs

1 pound beef sirloin cut in 1-inch
cubes (16 pieces)
½ cup dry red wine
1 medium clove garlic, minced
⅛ teaspoon basil, crushed
1 tablespoon butter or margarine
1 can (10¾ ounces) condensed
golden mushroom soup

¼ cup ketchup
12 pieces green pepper
(1 inch)
12 cherry tomatoes
Salad oil

In deep bowl, combine meat and wine; refrigerate 2 hours. Drain, reserving wine. In saucepan, cook garlic and basil in butter; stir in soup, wine, and ketchup. Cook over low heat for 5 minutes. Stir occasionally. Arrange alternately on 4 skewers: beef, pepper, and tomatoes; brush lightly with oil. Place on grill 4 inches above glowing coals. Cook for 12 to 18 minutes turning and brushing frequently with sauce. Heat remaining sauce; serve over kabobs. 4 servings.

Beef on a Spit

1 can (10½ ounces) condensed
onion soup
½ soup can water
1 tablespoon blue cheese,
crumbled

3 to 4-pound top quality beef
rotisserie roast

In shallow baking dish, combine soup, water, and cheese; add beef. Marinate at room temperature for 2 hours; turn once. Save marinade. Mount and balance beef on spit. Insert meat thermometer into beef. Roast 1½ hours or until 130°F. (rare) on meat thermometer following oven manufacturer's directions. In saucepan, heat marinade until cheese is melted; stir occasionally. Thicken with 1 tablespoon flour if desired. Serve with meat. 6 to 8 servings.

Rotisserie Beef and Big Red Sauce

2 cans (10¾ ounces each)
   condensed tomato soup
2 tablespoons honey
2 tablespoons wine vinegar

1 medium clove garlic, minced
¼ teaspoon thyme, crushed
3 to 4-pound top quality beef
   rotisserie roast

In saucepan, combine all ingredients except roast. Cover; cook over low heat 10 minutes. Stir occasionally. Mount and balance beef on spit. Insert meat thermometer into beef. Roast 1½ hours or until 130°F. (rare) on meat thermometer following oven manufacturer's directions. Brush often with sauce the last 30 minutes. Heat remaining sauce; serve with meat. 6 to 8 servings.

Outdoor Method: Mount and balance beef on spit. Insert meat thermometer into beef. Place foil drip pan under meat to catch drippings. Place in barbecue rotisserie over glowing coals. Roast 1½ hours or until 130°F. (rare) on meat thermometer. Brush often with sauce the last 30 minutes. Heat remaining sauce; serve with meat.

London Broil Exceptionale

1 can (10¾ ounces) condensed
   tomato soup
⅓ cup Burgundy or other dry
   red wine
2 tablespoons finely chopped
   ripe olives

1 small clove garlic, minced
1 tablespoon finely chopped
   onion
1½-pound flank steak, scored

In shallow baking dish, combine all ingredients except steak. Add steak. Marinate at room temperature 1 hour turning once. Transfer steak to broiler pan. In saucepan, cook marinade covered over low heat 10 minutes; stir occasionally. Broil steak 4 inches from heat about 4 minutes on each side or until desired doneness, brushing with sauce. Heat remaining sauce; serve with steak. 6 servings.

Outdoor Method: Proceed as above. Cook 4 inches above glowing coals 5 minutes on each side, brushing with sauce. Serve with remaining sauce.

Oniony Barbecued Burgers

⅓ cup finely chopped celery
1 tablespoon butter or margarine
1 tablespoon flour
1 can (10½ ounces) condensed
   onion soup

¼ cup ketchup
¼ cup water
1 tablespoon prepared horseradish
¼ teaspoon Worcestershire

In saucepan, cook celery in butter until tender. Add flour. Gradually stir in remaining ingredients. Cook, stirring until thickened. Makes about 1½ cups sauce. Serve as barbecue sauce for hamburgers or steak, following Indoor or Outdoor Methods p. 112 and 113.

SAUCES

The triumph of many of our most favored dishes may be attributed to the selection of the sauce. Sauces enhance many foods by imparting desirable flavors to them, and by making them more attractive.

Contrary to the belief of many cooks who have tried to master the art of sauce preparation, however, there is no sorcery involved. Today sauce-making is quite easy in contrast to what Brillat-Savarin wrote some years ago: "One can learn to cook, and one can be taught to roast, but a good sauce-maker is a genius born, not made." In the realm of *haute cuisine*, particularly that developed by the French, the intricate and lengthy technique of making refined sauces was not easily acquired.

But now, happily you have superb sauces at your fingertips in versatile condensed soups.

These soups have the delicate extra seasoning and ingredients that make them excellent sauces as they come from the can. For example, cream of chicken or cream of mushroom which go so well with many meats and vegetables. Golden mushroom soup blends the elegance of wine and herbs with beef stock, resulting in mushroom sauce par excellence.

With the repertoire of basic soup-sauces and many savory variations, you are prepared to offer family and guests the best of these specialties.

❋ *Bearnaise Sauce*

*2 tablespoons chopped shallots
    or onions*
¼ teaspoon tarragon, crushed
2 tablespoons butter or margarine
*½ cup Sauterne or other dry
    white wine*

½ teaspoon tarragon vinegar
*1 can (10¾ ounces) condensed
    cream of celery soup*
2 egg yolks

In saucepan, cook shallots and tarragon in butter until shallots are tender. Add wine and vinegar; simmer a few minutes. Remove from heat. Stir in soup and egg yolks. Cook over low heat, stirring constantly until thickened. Makes about 1½ cups sauce. Serve over sliced cooked beef, or broiled fish.

❋ *Souper Gravy*
For beef, chicken, pork, potatoes, noodles, or rice

*1 can (10¾ ounces) condensed
    cream of celery, chicken,
    mushroom or golden
    mushroom soup*

2 to 4 tablespoons water
*2 to 4 tablespoons drippings
    or butter*

When preparing gravy for roast or fried meat, remove meat from pan and pour off and measure drippings. Pour can of soup into pan; stir well to loosen browned bits. Blend in water and drippings. Heat; stir often. Makes about 1½ cups gravy.

Golden Sour Cream Sauce

¼ cup chopped onion
½ teaspoon paprika
2 tablespoons butter or margarine

*1 can (10¾ ounces) condensed
    golden mushroom soup*
¼ cup sour cream

In saucepan, cook onion with paprika in butter until tender. Stir in soup and sour cream. Heat; stir occasionally. Makes 1½ cups sauce. Serve over sliced cooked beef, hamburgers, noodles, potatoes, or rice.

Three delectable fool-proof sauces: Hollandaise, Chasseur *and* Bearnaise. *Each adorns a treasured food and is prepared in minutes with condensed soup, a joy to many cooks.*

SAUCE CHART

❋ ***Basic Cream Sauce*** *(similar to Bechamel and Veloute)*

Serve with cooked vegetables.

Combine 1 can condensed cream of celery or chicken or mushroom soup with ¼ to ⅓ cup milk. Heat; stir. Makes 1½ cups.

Variations:

❋ ***Hollandaise Sauce*** To Basic Cream Sauce add 2 tablespoons each butter and lemon juice and 2 egg yolks, slightly beaten. Simmer until just thickened (about 5 minutes), stirring constantly. Makes 1¾ cups. Serve with cooked vegetables or fish.

Mornay Sauce To Basic Cream Sauce add ½ cup shredded natural Swiss cheese, 2 tablespoons grated Parmesan cheese. Heat until cheese melts; stir often. Makes 1½ cups. Serve over cooked meats, poultry, fish, vegetables, or poached eggs.

Onion Sauce Cook ½ cup chopped onion in 2 tablespoons butter until tender. Stir in ingredients for Basic Cream Sauce. Heat; stir. Serve over cooked meats, fish, or vegetables.

❋ ***Sour Cream Sauce*** Cook ¼ cup chopped onion in 1 tablespoon butter until tender. Stir in Basic Cream Sauce, substituting ½ cup sour cream for milk in Basic Cream Sauce recipe, and ⅛ teaspoon paprika. Heat; stir. Makes 2 cups. Serve with cooked noodles, meats, or poultry.

❋ ***Basic Tomato Sauce***

Serve with cooked fish and meat.

Combine 1 can (10¾ ounces) condensed tomato soup with 2 tablespoons water. Heat; stir. Makes 1¼ cups.

Variations: To Basic Tomato Sauce add *any one* of the following before heating:

⅛ teaspoon crushed basil or oregano.

¼ teaspoon crushed dried dill weed.

1 tablespoon capers.

2 tablespoons chopped parsley or ripe olives.

1 teaspoon prepared mustard.

Substitute sour cream for water.

2 teaspoons Worcestershire or prepared horseradish.

❈ *Basic Cheddar Cheese Sauce*

Serve with cooked fish, meat, omelets, poultry, or vegetables.

Combine 1 can condensed Cheddar cheese soup with ¼ to ⅓ cup milk. Heat; stir. Makes 1½ cups.

Variations: To Basic Cheese Sauce add *any one* of the following before heating:

1 tablespoon chili sauce or ketchup.

2 tablespoons chopped parsley.

Generous dash crushed dried dill weed or nutmeg.

Substitute sour cream for milk.

❈ *Basic Golden Mushroom Sauce*

Serve with cooked meats, noodles, potatoes, poultry, or rice.

Combine 1 can condensed golden mushroom soup with ⅓ cup water. Heat; stir. Makes 1½ cups.

Variations:

Bordelaise Sauce Cook ¼ cup chopped onion or shallots in 2 tablespoons butter. Add ¼ cup dry red wine; simmer a few minutes. Stir in Golden Mushroom Sauce, 1 tablespoon chopped parsley. Heat; stir. Makes 2 cups. Serve over cooked meats, poultry, or vegetables.

Chasseur Sauce Cook 2 tablespoons sliced green onion or chopped shallots with dash crushed tarragon in 1 tablespoon butter until onion is tender. Add ¼ cup dry white wine; simmer a few minutes. Stir in Golden Mushroom Sauce, 2 tablespoons chopped canned tomato, and 1 tablespoon finely chopped parsley. Heat; stir. Makes 1⅔ cups. Serve with cooked meats or poultry.

Espagnole Sauce Cook 1 slice bacon; remove and crumble. Add ⅓ cup chopped onion, 1 small bay leaf, and ⅛ teaspoon crushed thyme to drippings; cook until onion is tender. Stir in Golden Mushroom Sauce, ⅓ cup tomato juice, and reserved bacon. Heat; stir. Makes 2 cups. Serve with cooked meats, poultry, or vegetables.

Herb Sauce Cook ⅓ cup chopped onion or shallots in 2 tablespoons butter until tender. Add ¼ cup dry white wine; simmer a few minutes. Stir in Golden Mushroom Sauce, 1 tablespoon chopped parsley, and generous dash each crushed chervil and tarragon. Heat; stir. Makes 2 cups. Serve over cooked meats, poultry, or vegetables.

Madeira Sauce Simmer ¼ cup Madeira wine a few minutes. Stir in Golden Mushroom Sauce. Heat; stir. Makes 1⅔ cups. Serve over cooked meats or poultry.

Lyonnaise Sauce Cook 1 cup chopped onion in 3 tablespoons butter until tender. Add ¼ cup dry white wine; simmer a few minutes. Stir in Golden Mushroom Sauce. Heat; stir. Makes 2 cups. Serve with cooked meats, poultry, or vegetables.

ENTERTAINING
for Family and Friends

Social gatherings have essentially the same purpose at your house and mine — to express the spirit of hospitality. The pleasant memory of the guest is the host or hostess' reward. A common bond of all of us is this desire to welcome family and friends with good taste and versatility. The occasion may include a few or many persons, may be simple or elegant, with little or much fine fare.

To maintain hospitable standards in today's hectic world, however, requires some forethought. If you're an experienced host or hostess, you may well know the problems of coping with your various roles as shopper, planner, cook and director. If you're less experienced, perhaps newly married, you may just now be confronted with creating, planning and performing the varied chores attendant on your new status. All of us, however, welcome proven ideas and imaginative suggestions to make our social events distinctive and individual.

In offering here some helpful hints, creative menus and reliable recipes for a variety of occasions, the aim is to inspire not restrict, for each individual will interpret them differently. By simplifying your approach, however, you'll find that hospitality need be neither hectic nor haphazard.

Plan the event, organize your resources, take advantage of the excellent and varied convenience foods the modern world affords, and, above all, prepare as much of the fare as possible beforehand. You'll be calm and composed — no furrowed brow — when your guests arrive.

Planning the Party
What Is The Occasion? There are many reasons and times for entertaining. It may be a party to welcome neighbors, celebrate a birthday, greet old

friends, salute a co-worker. To vary the usual luncheons and dinners, dream up a theme to make the party memorable. Invite guests to come in costume, perhaps for a Mexican Fiesta or plan a Continental Buffet.

What Kind Of A Party? Before deciding the kind of party and how many persons to invite, consider your entertaining facilities. The seating and serving space will influence the number.

The Menu: In selecting the menu, plan on dishes which you know. Choose foods which can be partially or completely prepared ahead. In general, it is advisable to avoid exotic foods. A simple, but good, menu is often preferable to the more elaborate one.

Service: The best and easiest way to serve company depends on your home and equipment. Perhaps you find buffet parties go most smoothly; however, this requires trays or tray tables. Some find it handier to use the traditional "at table" approach with the host doing the honors in serving the main course to each guest while the hostess adds accompaniments.

Preparing The Food: Cook beforehand as much of the menu as possible. Some dishes can be frozen well in advance. Others will keep overnight in the refrigerator. Leave only what is absolutely necessary for the day of the party. Calculate the cooking times for any dishes which have to be done after guests arrive so everything is ready at once. Be sure you have not counted on using one oven for dishes which take different temperatures.

The Day of the Party

In The Morning: Check all the details of the party. Has the ice been made? Is there a place for coats? Have the necessary serving dishes and utensils been gathered?

At The Party: After the guests arrive, relax and enjoy yourself, while you are keeping an eye on what is going on. Try to serve the meal on schedule. If unexpected crises arise, take them in good stride. Above all, plan so you can enjoy your guests and so they enjoy your hospitality.

The following menus give a variety of suggestions for brunches, luncheons, and dinners. Asterisks mark the menu items for which there are recipes.

Brunch Elegante

In New Orleans, 'tis the late-morning custom to dine elegantly and leisurely at brunch, beginning with a favorite "eye-opener" and concluding with hot strong coffee. The meal may be enjoyed on a flower-decorated patio or inside. But guests will welcome a gay and pretty setting. For a color theme, use a pastel cloth or mats and napkins. The fruit course can be a spectacular centerpiece if you serve it in a hollowed small watermelon; dice the pink melon to mix with the oranges and berries; then heap in the green shell. Or you may prefer to serve individual halves of cantaloupe filled with other fruits. If you serve Eggs Benedict, you may want to use toasted English muffin halves as the base. Or if the chicken dish is your choice, remember the excellent frozen patty shells. The regal cake winds up the repast in fitting style and is not too sweet.

Chilled Fresh Orange Slices with Berries

Eggs Benedict* or Chicken and Eggs Francoise*

Angelfood Cake with Chocolate Glaze

Milk or Coffee

❋ *Eggs Benedict*

1 can (10¾ ounces) condensed
   cream of celery, chicken, or
   mushroom soup
⅓ cup milk

6 thin slices ham, fried
6 slices buttered toast
6 eggs, poached
1 tablespoon finely chopped parsley

In saucepan, blend soup and milk. Heat; stir occasionally. Meanwhile, place a slice of ham on each slice of toast; top with a poached egg. Pour sauce over eggs. Garnish with parsley. 6 servings.

Chicken and Eggs Francoise

1 can (2 ounces) whole mushrooms,
   drained
⅛ teaspoon thyme, crushed
4 tablespoons butter or margarine
1 can (10¾ ounces) condensed
   cream of celery soup
¾ cup light cream or milk

1 cup cubed cooked chicken
2 tablespoons chopped pimiento
4 eggs, slightly beaten
¼ teaspoon salt
4 patty shells
Chopped parsley

In saucepan, brown mushrooms with thyme in 2 tablespoons butter until tender. Add soup, ½ cup cream, chicken, and pimiento. Heat; stir occasionally. Meanwhile, combine eggs, salt, and ¼ cup cream. In skillet, gently scramble eggs in 2 tablespoons butter. Layer eggs and creamed chicken in patty shells. Garnish with parsley. 4 servings.

Continental Luncheon

In Rome, Vienna, Boston or Omaha, a week-day luncheon is a happy occasion for women friends to gather and enjoy a few hours of leisure and good talk. Welcome your guests to an imaginative setting using pretty linens, china, and an artistic centerpiece. For canapes, place a slice of cucumber on each buttered round of white bread; garnish with a dab of mayonnaise and chopped chives; refrigerate. The crepes can be prepared and frozen beforehand. Thaw and fill before the party. Sprinkle the tomatoes with oil, vinegar, fresh herbs, salt and pepper; refrigerate. The souffle can be made the day before.

Cucumber Canapes with Cups of Hot Beef Broth

Shrimp and Ham in Patty Shells* or Crepes a la Reine*

Tomato Slices Vinaigrette

Cold Lemon Souffle

Cafe au Lait

❋ *Shrimp and Ham in Patty Shells*

1 cup ham strips
2 cups sliced mushrooms
(about 1/2 pound)
1 medium clove garlic, minced
1/4 cup butter or margarine

2 cans (10¾ ounces each) condensed cream of chicken soup
1/2 cup light cream
2 cups cooked shrimp
1/4 cup chopped parsley
Patty shells

In saucepan, brown ham and cook mushrooms and garlic in butter. Stir in soup and cream. Add shrimp and parsley. Heat; stir occasionally. Serve in patty shells. Makes about 5 cups.

Crepes a la Reine

Crepes:

2 eggs, slightly beaten
1 cup milk
2/3 cup flour

1 tablespoon salad oil
1/2 teaspoon salt

Filling and sauce:

1 1/2 cups chopped mushrooms
(about 1/4 pound)
1 cup chopped celery
1/4 cup chopped onion
1/8 teaspoon thyme, crushed
1/4 cup butter or margarine
1 can (10¾ ounces) condensed cream of chicken soup

1 1/2 cups chopped cooked chicken
1/4 teaspoon salt
Dash pepper
1/4 cup light cream
2 tablespoons Sauterne or other dry white wine

To make crepes: In bowl, with rotary beater, beat crepe ingredients until smooth. To make each crepe, in hot, lightly oiled skillet (6-inch diameter), pour about 2 tablespoons batter, tilting pan slightly to quickly spread batter thinly and evenly. Lightly brown first side; turn and cook second side a few seconds. Make 12 crepes. Hold on heated platter.

To make filling: In skillet, brown mushrooms and cook celery and onion with thyme in butter until tender. Stir in 1/4 cup soup, chicken, salt, and pepper. Heat, stirring. Spoon about 3 tablespoons filling on each crepe; roll up. **To make sauce:** In saucepan, combine remaining soup, cream, and Sauterne. Heat; stir occasionally. Spoon sauce over crepes; serve immediately. Makes 6 servings.

Soup and Sandwich Times

Teenagers' Pre-Shopping Lunch

Give added pizazz to the usual without going too unusual; toss in the convenience of out-of-hand eating and you have the necessary formula for feeding a teen.

Mugs of Green Pea Soup or Chicken Vegetable Soup
Party-Burgers*
Orange Sherbet

Party-Burgers

Prepare Cheeseburgers as usual. Top each with a kabob of nibblers — pickle chips, olives, tomato wedges.

Lunch for Grandmother's Friends

Set a frilly table complete with the best china, and tea roses in a crystal vase to complement a fancy menu.

Cups of Hot Tomato Chantilly*
Minced Chicken and Salmon
Finger Sandwiches
Cranberry Relish on Lettuce
Brownies a la Mode
Hot Tea

Tomato Chantilly

1 can (10¾ ounces) condensed   Whipped cream
   tomato soup   Nutmeg
1 soup can water

In saucepan, combine soup and water. Heat; stir occasionally. Meanwhile, place about 1 teaspoon whipped cream in each cup or mug; sprinkle with nutmeg. Pour hot soup over; serve immediately. Makes about 2½ cups.

Golfers' Get-Together

Whether your "pro" gets the trophy or finishes last in the day's tournament, he'll know he's got a winner when you offer him this man-pleasing reward.

Cream of Potato Soup or Clam Chowder with Croutons
Reuben Sandwiches
(Corned Beef, Sauerkraut, and Swiss Cheese on Rye Bread)
Pickles and Radishes
Tray of Assorted Cookies and Fruit
Iced Coffee

Soup and Salad Times

A Hot-Weather Lunch

Refresh your salad days with a cup or bowl of chilled soup eaten alfresco. Invite the back-fence neighbors over to make lunch an occasion.

Chilled Cream of Asparagus Soup with Sour Cream
Chicken-Orange Salad in Orange Shells*
Crusty Rolls
Nut Cookies
Milk or Iced Coffee

Chicken-Orange Salad

Toss together cooked cubed chicken, orange sections, and celery with a light dressing.

Christmas Luncheon

Greet guests in the living room with a cup of warming soup to "sip and spoon" (it will keep hot in a chafing dish or in a handsome heat-proof casserole on a warming tray).

Cups of Chicken Rice or Turkey Vegetable Soup
Ribbon Aspic* *(see index)*
Mince Pie or Fruit Cake and Ice Cream
Hot Spiced Tea or Coffee

An Easy Sunday Lunch

To fill the bill for a day of relaxation — make the salads a day ahead and add shelf handy canned items.

Cups of Black Bean Soup with Lemon Slices
Ham-and-Egg Salad*
Toast or Melba Toast Rounds
Rice Pudding*
Milk or Hot Coffee

Ham-and-Egg Salad

Mix strips of ham with sliced hard-cooked eggs, celery, and mayonnaise. Serve in lettuce cups.

Rice Pudding

Buy prepared pudding. Spoon into sherbet glasses; top with strawberry jam and chopped pecans.

Autumn-Winter Luncheon for Men

A gathering of men for any occasion is an opportunity to enjoy the German spirit of *Gemutlichkeit*, a convivial celebration with good food and drinks. You can prepare this fare and set the whole meal, except dessert, on a buffet to let each man help himself. The host can ladle the soup into mugs or cups from a tureen or bowl. Slice the meat in the kitchen beforehand. Use the potato puffs and turnovers that come frozen to be heated in the oven.

German Sauerbraten

4-pound rump roast	*6 whole peppercorns*
1 can (10½ ounces) condensed onion soup	*10 whole cloves*
¾ cup wine vinegar	*2 tablespoons shortening*
½ cup water	*¼ cup sugar*
3 medium bay leaves	*½ cup crumbled ginger snaps (about 7)*

Place meat in deep bowl. Combine soup, vinegar, water, bay, peppercorns, and cloves; pour over meat. Cover, refrigerate for 2 days, turning meat twice each day. Remove meat from marinade. In large heavy pan, brown meat in shortening; pour off fat. Stir in marinade. Cover; cook over low heat 2½ hours or until tender. Remove meat from pan; keep warm. Skim fat from gravy; remove bay, peppercorns, and cloves. Stir in sugar and ginger snaps. Cook until thickened, stirring. Serve with meat. 6 to 8 servings.

The Committee Luncheon

This menu is delightful to serve buffet-style. Fill sherbet glasses or cups with Herbed Tomato Slush or Consomme Parfait; garnish with yogurt and chopped chives, or watercress or dill; refrigerate. Pass to guests before the meal. The attractive chicken dish can be partially prepared beforehand and baked after the guests arrive. For decor, feature the colors of nature (which are Danish favorites), green and blue with white. Serve luncheon in keeping with the Danish *Velbekomme*, "May this meal become you well."

Herbed Tomato Slush

1 tablespoon finely chopped onion	*1 can (10¾ ounces) condensed tomato soup*
⅛ teaspoon marjoram, crushed	*1 soup can water*
⅛ teaspoon tarragon, crushed	*1 tablespoon lemon juice*
1 tablespoon butter or margarine	

In saucepan, cook onion with marjoram and tarragon in butter until tender. Stir in remaining ingredients. Pour into shallow pan. Freeze until partially frozen (about 3 hours); stir a few times. Break up with fork; spoon into sherbet glasses or bowls. Makes about 2½ cups.

Bring-the-Children Brunch

At a brunch after church or a lazy morning, parents and the younger set can all relax. The children may sit together at a small table, prettily decorated with paper appointments, while the grown-ups dine elsewhere. First serve juices and coffee from a cart as a welcoming note. Mix and shape the meat beforehand and bake after the guests arrive (takes only 20 minutes). Have the prepared vegetable platter (cucumbers, green peppers, carrots and celery) in the refrigerator.

Beef 'n Frank Wagon Wheel

1 can (10¾ ounces) condensed
   tomato soup
1½ pounds ground beef
1 teaspoon salt
1½ teaspoon chili powder
6 frankfurters, split

½ cup chopped onion
2 tablespoons
   butter or margarine
½ cup shredded process
   cheese
Grated Parmesan cheese

Place a double layer of foil on cookie sheet. Mix thoroughly ⅓ cup soup, beef, salt, and 1 teaspoon chili powder; pat out firmly into 11-inch circle about ½ inch thick on foil. Turn up edges of foil to catch fat. Firmly press frankfurters, cut side up, into meat in spoke fashion. In saucepan, cook onion with remaining chili in butter until tender; stir in remaining soup; spread over meat. Bake at 450°F. for 15 minutes. Spoon off fat. Sprinkle with cheeses; bake until melted. 6 servings.

Indoor-Outdoor Summertime Lunch

On a hot Sunday or summer holiday, some of us wish to dine leisurely outdoors but others prefer the comfort of a cooler indoor party. For either, summertime fare is superb. The cool Vichyssoise and aspic can be already prepared in the refrigerator. For the asparagus, saute ½ cup slivered almonds in ½ cup butter until golden; add 2 tablespoons lemon juice, salt and pepper; pour over hot cooked asparagus (2 pounds raw). Have the dessert ready in the refrigerator.

Calico Beef Aspic

1 can (10½ ounces) condensed
   beef broth
1 package (3 ounces)
   lemon-flavored gelatin
½ cup cold water
1 tablespoon grated onion

1 tablespoon vinegar
Dash salt
Dash pepper
1 cup diced cooked beef
⅓ cup diced red apple
2 tablespoons sliced celery

In saucepan, bring beef broth to a boil. Add gelatin; stir to dissolve. Add water, onion, vinegar, salt, and pepper. Chill until slightly thickened. Fold in remaining ingredients. Pour into a 3-cup mold. Chill until firm (about 4 hours). Garnish with hard-cooked egg wedges. Makes about 2½ cups.

Chilled Fruit Juices
**Beef 'n Frank
Wagon Wheel***
**Raw Vegetable Platter —
Mustard, Mayonnaise**
Hot Buttered Toast
Jam   Jelly
Sugared Doughnuts
Cold Milk   Coffee

Vichyssoise*
(see index)
Calico Beef Aspic*
Asparagus Amandine
Hot Biscuits
Butter   Marmalade
Fresh Pineapple Wedges
Coffee — Iced or Hot

Oyster Stew

Stuffed Turkey with Holiday Sauce* **(Garnish with Grape Clusters)**

Acorn Squash Rings

Glazed Carrots and Brussels Sprouts*

Jellied Vegetable Salad

Orange Bread

Ice Cream Balls with Egg Nog Sauce or Plum Pudding with Hard Sauce

Hot Tea or Coffee

Memorable Christmas Dinner

An important consideration for Christmas dinner is to plan one which will leave you time to enjoy the day's festivities. For the merry yuletide feast is a happy event to be shared with family and friends. Prepare much of the menu beforehand. Buy canned oyster stew. Have the salad ready in the refrigerator. The acorn squash offers a change from the standard potatoes. Dessert may be pretty ice cream balls, frozen and ready to be served with bourbon-flavored or plain egg nog sauce, or the more traditional plum pudding which can be purchased.

Stuffed Turkey with Holiday Sauce

6 slices bacon

1 cup sliced celery

½ cup chopped onion

1 package (8 ounces) herb seasoned stuffing

2 cups coarse cornbread crumbs

1 can (10½ ounces) condensed chicken broth

1 egg, slightly beaten

10-pound turkey

1 can (10¾ ounces) condensed cream of mushroom soup

½ cup whole berry cranberry sauce

¼ cup orange juice

In skillet, cook bacon until crisp; remove and crumble. Pour off all but 2 tablespoons drippings. Cook celery and onion in drippings until tender. Toss lightly with stuffing, crumbs, broth, and egg. Fill cavity of turkey loosely with stuffing. Truss; place in roasting pan. Cover with aluminum foil. Roast at 325°F. for about 4 hours (25 minutes per pound or until tender). Uncover last hour to brown. Remove turkey to serving platter. Skim fat from drippings; add remaining ingredients. Heat; stir to loosen browned bits. 8 servings.

❊ *Glazed Carrots and Brussels Sprouts*
Pictured on front cover

1 pound carrots, cut in 1½-inch pieces

2 packages (10 ounces each) frozen Brussels sprouts

2 tablespoons chopped onion

2 tablespoons butter or margarine

1 can (10½ ounces) condensed consomme

⅓ cup apple juice

2 teaspoons lemon juice

2 tablespoons cornstarch

1 tablespoon brown sugar

Generous dash ground clove

Cook carrots and Brussels sprouts; drain. Meanwhile, in saucepan, cook onion in butter until tender. Add remaining ingredients. Cook, stirring until thickened. Combine with hot vegetables. Makes about 4 cups.

This Christmas Dinner coasts into the spotlight carrying a luscious trio of buttery Oyster Stew, *squash and* Stuffed Turkey with Holiday Sauce.

Pork Dinner for New Year's

The world's oldest holiday, and the only one celebrated by all peoples everywhere, is most happily spent mixing convivially with friends or relatives. You may wish to promote this harmonious spirit by entertaining with an inviting dinner during the day or in the evening. It is a pleasing variation to include dishes which are not traditional for the "Twelve Days of Christmas." This pork dinner is such an innovation.

Bullshot

Fill an old fashioned glass with ice cubes. Add 1 ounce vodka. Pour in 4 ounces (½ cup) undiluted beef broth. Garnish with slice of lemon. 1 serving.

Bully Scotch Sipper

3½ ounces condensed beef broth   1 ounce Scotch

Fill an 8-ounce old fashioned glass with ice cubes. Add beef broth and Scotch. Stir. Garnish with lemon peel. Serve with celery stick stirrer. 1 serving.

❋ Party Cheese Logs

1 can (11½ ounces) condensed   2 tablespoons Worcestershire
  bean with bacon soup   1 medium clove garlic, minced
4 cups (1 pound) shredded   ½ teaspoon hot pepper sauce
  sharp Cheddar cheese   Chopped walnuts or parsley
½ cup finely chopped onion

In large bowl of electric mixer, combine all ingredients except walnuts. Beat on low speed until *smooth*. Chill; divide mixture in half. On waxed paper, shape each half into a log (8x1½ inches); roll in walnuts. Refrigerate. Serve logs as a spread for breads or crackers. Makes 2 logs.

Glazed Pork Loin

4-pound loin of pork   2 tablespoons lemon juice
⅓ cup chopped celery   2 tablespoons brown sugar
1 tablespoon butter or margarine   1 tablespoon cornstarch
1 can (10½ ounces) condensed   ¼ teaspoon dry mustard
  consomme   Generous dash cinnamon

In roasting pan, roast meat fat side up at 325°F. for about 2½ hours (35 to 40 minutes per pound or 170°F. on meat thermometer). Meanwhile, in saucepan, cook celery in butter until tender; add remaining ingredients. Cook over low heat, stirring until thickened. During last 30 minutes of roasting time, brush roast frequently with sauce. Heat remaining sauce; serve with roast. 6 to 8 servings.

Festive Easter Dinner

With spring in the air and everyone in good spirits, the delights of Easter are many. A most enjoyable way of celebrating the holiday is with a pleasing Sunday dinner served at a festive table. Make a centerpiece of colored Easter eggs or with spring flowers. Perhaps the meal will precede or follow an indoor or outdoor egg hunt. Or, in the Greek tradition, begin the meal with the ancient custom of egg cracking. Each person tries to crack the tip of a hard-cooked egg held tightly in the hand of the person next to him. When all are cracked, best wishes are exchanged. This menu of familiar dishes can be enjoyed at leisure.

**"V-8" Cocktail
Vegetable Juice
Curried Stuffed Eggs
Mint-glazed Leg of Lamb*
Scalloped Potatoes* or
Parsleyed New Potatoes
Buttered Fresh Broccoli
Lettuce with Herb Dressing
Hot Nut Muffins
Strawberry Ice Cream Pie**

Mint-glazed Leg of Lamb

4 to 5-pound leg of lamb
¼ cup chopped onion
1 small clove garlic, minced
1 tablespoon butter or margarine
1 can (10½ ounces)
  condensed consomme

½ cup mint-flavored
  apple jelly
5 teaspoons cornstarch
1 tablespoon lemon juice

Remove fell from lamb (parchment-like covering); trim excess fat. Place on rack in shallow baking dish, fat side up. Roast at 325°F. until done (30 to 35 minutes per pound or 175°F. on meat thermometer). Meanwhile, in saucepan, cook onion with garlic in butter until tender; add remaining ingredients. Cook over low heat, stirring until thickened. Brush lamb with sauce during last 30 minutes. Heat remaining sauce; serve with lamb. 4 to 6 servings.

❊ *Scalloped Potatoes*

1 can (10¾ ounces) condensed
  cream of celery
  or mushroom soup
⅓ to ½ cup milk
¼ cup chopped parsley
Dash pepper

4 cups thinly sliced raw
  potatoes
1 small onion, thinly sliced
1 tablespoon
  butter or margarine
Dash paprika

Combine soup, milk, parsley, and pepper. In a buttered 1½-quart casserole, arrange alternate layers of potatoes, onion, and sauce. Dot top with butter; sprinkle with paprika. Cover; bake at 375°F. for 1 hour. Uncover; bake 15 minutes more or until potatoes are done. Makes about 3½ cups.

V. I. P. Dinner

On that special occasion when you wish to serve a sit-down dinner with gracious elegance and your best appointments, this menu matches the mood. For the decor, select a single color to accent in napkins and candles — perhaps royal blue. Use place cards, and attach a fresh flower blossom to each napkin. For salad, cook small carrots; chill; and cover with sour cream.

Chilled Minted Pea Soup
Recipe may be doubled

1 can (11¼ ounces) condensed
   green pea soup
1 soup can milk

¼ cup light cream
½ teaspoon dried mint flakes,
   crushed

Blend all ingredients. Chill at least 4 hours. Makes about 2½ cups.

❋ Stuffed Beef Roll

1½ pounds round steak (about
   ¼ inch thick), trimmed
¼ pound ground veal
1 egg, slightly beaten
¼ cup small bread cubes
2 tablespoons grated Parmesan cheese
2 slices (2 ounces) salami,
   cut in strips
2 slices (2 ounces) Provolone
   cheese, cut in strips

2 hard-cooked eggs, sliced
2 tablespoons shortening
1 can (10¾ ounces)
   condensed tomato soup
½ cup water
½ cup chopped onion
¼ cup Burgundy or other
   dry red wine
1 medium clove garlic, minced
1 small bay leaf

Pound steak. Combine veal, egg, bread, and Parmesan cheese. Spread mixture evenly on steak to within 1 inch of edges. Press salami, Provolone cheese, and sliced eggs into meat mixture. Starting at narrow end, roll up; tuck in ends. Tie with string or fasten with skewers. In skillet, brown roll in shortening; pour off fat. Add remaining ingredients. Cover; cook over low heat 1 hour. Turn; cook 1 hour more. Stir occasionally. Remove bay leaf. 6 servings.

❋ Pilaf
Recipe may be doubled

½ cup fine noodles, broken
   in pieces
2 tablespoons butter or margarine

1 can (10¾ ounces)
   condensed chicken broth
⅓ cup water
½ cup raw regular rice

In saucepan, brown noodles in butter; stir often. Add remaining ingredients. Bring to a boil; stir. Cover; cook over low heat 20 to 25 minutes or until liquid is absorbed. Makes about 2 cups.

Fun with Fondue

The serving of Beef Fondue Bourguignonne is a friendly meal with everyone seated around the cooking dish. Each person cooks the meat in hot oil in the fondue pot or chafing dish according to individual preference. Then the beef is dunked in one or more flavorful sauces. It is preferable to have long-handled forks for the cooking of the beef. You may vary the accompaniments as desired but they are generally light fare. Glasses of red wine often are served with the fondue.

Fondue Bourguignonne*
Assorted Sauces*
Individual Green Salads
French Bread
Melon with Lime or Mint Ice Cream
Coffee

❋ *Fondue Bourguignonne*

*1 can (10¾ ounces) condensed
    cream of celery soup*

*2 pounds sirloin steak or filet
    mignon*
Vegetable oil

Using soup, prepare any combination of sauces listed below. Cut meat into ¾-inch cubes; trim all fat. Refrigerate until 30 minutes before serving. Half fill fondue saucepot with oil; heat until oil is gently bubbling. Spear meat with fondue forks. Cook until desired doneness (about 1 minute). Transfer meat to plate; dip into a choice of sauces. 4 servings.

Sauces:

For each sauce, mix ingredients listed in small serving dishes (about ½ cup size).

Curry Sauce:

*⅓ can condensed cream of celery
    soup (about ⅓ cup)*

2 tablespoons mayonnaise
1 teaspoon curry powder

Serve with dishes of toasted coconut and chopped chutney.

Mock Bearnaise Sauce:

*⅓ can condensed cream of celery
    soup (about ⅓ cup)*

2 tablespoons mayonnaise
1 tablespoon tarragon vinegar
1 teaspoon chervil, crushed

Horseradish Sauce:

*⅓ can condensed cream of celery
    soup (about ⅓ cup)*

2 tablespoons sour cream
1 tablespoon prepared horseradish

Serve with a small dish of finely chopped green onion.

Italian Trattoria Buffet

Serve this delightful menu buffet-style to guests who will sit at small tables, covered with informal cloths and colorful appointments in the style of an Italian trattoria, rustic restaurant. To make the antipasti salad, arrange on a bed of greens a variety of olives, sardines, tuna, artichoke hearts, pickled peppers, salami slices, hard-cooked egg wedges and marinated mushrooms. Prepare beforehand and chill. The manicotti can be partly prepared ahead of time and baked after the guests arrive. Serve chianti wine with dinner, and make Espresso for a grand finale.

Minestrone au Pistou*
Antipasti Salad
Manicotti*
Braised Zucchini
Bread Sticks
Fresh Fruit and Cheese
Espresso Coffee

Minestrone au Pistou

1 medium clove garlic, minced
1 teaspoon basil, crushed
2 tablespoons grated
  Parmesan cheese
1 teaspoon tomato paste

1 tablespoon olive oil
2 cans (10½ ounces each)
  condensed minestrone soup
2 soup cans water

Using a bowl and wooden spoon (or a mortar and pestle), pound garlic and basil into a paste. Blend in cheese and tomato paste. Add oil. In saucepan, heat soup and water. Stir garlic mixture into soup. Serve with additional cheese. Makes about 5 cups.

Manicotti

8 manicotti (about ¼ pound)
  macaroni
2 cups (1 pound) dry cottage
  cheese
1 egg, slightly beaten
⅓ cup grated Parmesan cheese
¼ cup finely chopped parsley
½ pound ground beef
⅓ cup chopped onion

2 medium cloves garlic, minced
1 teaspoon basil, crushed
1 teaspoon oregano, crushed
2 cans (10¾ ounces each)
  condensed tomato soup
½ cup water
2 slices (3 ounces) Mozzarella
  cheese, cut into 8 triangles

Cook manicotti until tender; drain. Combine cottage cheese, egg, Parmesan, and parsley; fill manicotti. Arrange manicotti in shallow baking dish (12x8x2 inches). In saucepan, brown meat and cook onion, garlic, basil, and oregano until onion is tender. Stir in soup and water. Pour over manicotti. Bake at 350°F. for 35 minutes. Top with Mozzarella. Bake until cheese melts. 4 servings.

An Italian Trattoria Buffet is a fun and informal party
featuring Manicotti *and* Antipasti Salad.

141

Royal Hawaiian Luau

Transport your guests to the charming informality of Hawaii with this appealing menu. The entertaining area can become a tropical garden with greenery, potted plants and fresh flowers. Use colorful lanterns. Decorate the table with green leaves and a centerpiece of fresh fruit (including pineapples). Ask everyone to come in island costume — slacks and bright aloha shirts for men, and mumuus for the women. Give paper or flower leis to each guest. Don't forget lyrical Hawaiian music. Allow sufficient time to make the delectable main dish and Rumaki.

Rumaki

1 package (8 ounces) frozen
   chicken livers
3 tablespoons soy sauce

Dash ginger
1 tablespoon sugar
6 water chestnuts, quartered
12 slices bacon, cut in half

Thaw livers as directed on package; cut into 24 pieces. Combine soy, ginger, and sugar; marinate livers in mixture for 30 minutes at room temperature. Drain. Fold a piece of liver over water chestnut. Wrap bacon around liver; fasten with toothpick. Bake in pan on rack at 350°F. for 35 minutes or until bacon is crisp. Makes 24 appetizers.

Turban of Flounder, Macadamia

1 cup sliced celery
3 tablespoons butter or margarine
2 cans (10¾ ounces each)
   condensed chicken broth
⅓ cup raw regular rice
2 cups diced cooked shrimp
½ cup drained pineapple tidbits

8 thin fillets of flounder
   (about 2 pounds)
¼ cup sliced green onion
2 tablespoons sherry
¼ cup chopped Macadamia nuts
1 tablespoon chopped pimiento
2 tablespoons cornstarch

In saucepan, cook celery in 2 tablespoons butter until tender. Add ¾ cup broth and the rice. Bring to a boil. Cover; cook over low heat 20 minutes or until all liquid is absorbed. Add shrimp and pineapple. Line a 5-cup well-buttered ring mold with fish as follows: alternating wide and narrow ends, overlap fillets, and let ends hang over outside of mold; fill with shrimp mixture; fold fillet ends over top; place mold on baking sheet. Bake at 350°F. for 40 minutes. To pour off excess liquid, place cake rack over mold; invert but do not unmold. Unmold on serving platter. Meanwhile, in saucepan, cook onion in 1 tablespoon butter. Add 1 can broth, sherry, nuts and pimiento. Combine cornstarch with remaining broth (½ cup); stir into sauce. Cook, stirring until thickened. Serve over mold. 8 servings.

Parisian Dinner Menu

**Liver Pate* or
French Onion Soup***
(see index)
**Chicken Magnifique with
White and Wild Rice*
or Chicken in
Champagne Sauce***
French Peas
Croissants
**Cold Chocolate
Midnight Souffle**
Demitasse

When dining in gay Paree, you may sample elegant and complicated dishes amid regal surroundings or enjoy the pleasantries of robust country fare in an informal bistro. No matter the setting, the food will be honest and good, prepared with care and devotion. Your friends will be enchanted with this delightful dinner, planned with continental flair. For a French touch to frozen peas, add a little chopped lettuce, butter, pinch of sugar, salt and pepper to them while cooking. Chilled white wine may be served with the dinner. Prepare the chocolate souffle early in the day and refrigerate; for a midnight garnish, top with puffs of whipped cream plus tiny stars and a crescent moon cut from thin orange rind.

❈ *Chicken Magnifique*

*4 chicken breasts (about
  3 pounds), split*
¼ cup butter or margarine
*2 cups sliced mushrooms (about
  ½ pound)*
*2 cans (10¾ ounces each)
  condensed cream of chicken
  soup*

1 large clove garlic, minced
Generous dash crushed thyme
⅛ teaspoon rosemary, crushed
⅔ cup light cream
*2 packages (6 ounces each)
  long grain and wild rice mix,
  prepared*

Use 1 large skillet or prepare in 2 skillets (about 10 inches) by dividing the ingredients equally. Brown chicken in butter; remove. Brown mushrooms. Stir in soup, garlic, and seasonings; add chicken. Cover; cook over low heat 30 minutes or until chicken is tender. Stir occasionally. Blend in cream; heat slowly. Serve with rice. 8 servings.

Wine: Add ½ cup Sauterne or sherry with soup. Decrease light cream to ½ cup.

Chicken in Champagne Sauce

*5 chicken breasts (about
  4 pounds), split, skinned,
  and boned*
¼ cup butter or margarine
1 split (8 ounces) Champagne

*1 can (10¾ ounces) condensed
  cream of chicken soup*
*1 can (10¾ ounces) condensed
  cream of mushroom soup*
⅓ cup light cream
Chopped parsley

In skillet, lightly brown chicken in butter (about 5 minutes each side); remove. Add Champagne to skillet, stirring to loosen browned bits and cooking until ½ the original volume. Stir in soups and cream; add chicken. Cook over low heat 20 minutes. Stir occasionally. Garnish with parsley. 8 to 10 servings.

Spanish Summertime Buffet

The Spanish love to dine outdoors amid a gay and colorful atmosphere. Capture the true Spanish spirit for a lovely buffet party with vibrant colors such as red and black. Wrought iron items can be used. Serve the cold Gazpacho soup-salad in parfait glasses, cups, or bowls before the meal; the garnishes of chopped vegetables and croutons add to the delight of this dish. For the salad, slice large mild onions and oranges and sprinkle with oil and lemon juice. Prepare the custard in one large dish or smaller individual ones. Lively guitar or flamenco music in the background will add to the atmosphere.

❊ *Gazpacho*

2 medium cloves garlic, minced
2 tablespoons olive oil
3 cans (10¾ ounces each)
   condensed tomato soup
3 cups cold water

¼ cup wine vinegar
2 cups chopped cucumber
1 cup chopped green pepper
½ cup chopped onion
Croutons

In small saucepan, cook garlic in olive oil; combine in a large bowl with soup, water, and vinegar. Chill for 4 hours. Serve in chilled bowls. Pass chilled vegetables and croutons for garnish. Makes about 6½ cups.

Blender Version: Cook garlic as above. Combine in electric blender with 1 can soup, 1 cup water, ¼ cup cucumber, ¼ cup green pepper, 2 tablespoons onion, and 2 slices toast. Blend until smooth; combine in a large bowl with remaining soup, water, and vinegar. Chill as above. Garnish with remaining vegetables. Makes about 7 cups.

❊ *Spanish Paella*

3 pounds chicken parts
4 tablespoons salad oil
1 can (10¾ ounces) condensed
   tomato soup
1 can (10½ ounces) condensed
   onion soup
2½ soup cans water
4 medium cloves garlic, minced
2 teaspoons oregano, crushed

2 teaspoons salt
⅛ teaspoon pepper
2 pounds medium shrimp
   (about 36), cleaned
2 cups raw regular rice
2 large green peppers, cut in
   strips
1 cup chopped pimiento
⅔ cup sliced ripe olives

Use 1 large skillet or prepare in 2 skillets (about 10 inches), by dividing ingredients equally. Brown chicken in oil; pour off fat. Stir in soups, water, garlic, and seasonings. Cover; cook over low heat 15 minutes. Stir in remaining ingredients. Cook over low heat 30 minutes or until chicken and rice are tender. Stir occasionally. 8 to 10 servings.

For an occasion your guests will never forget, arrange a Spanish Summertime Buffet with cold Gazpacho soup and a sumptuous Paella.

Peanut Soup*
or Oyster Chowder*

Souperburgers*

Tossed Salad

Potato Chips or
French Fries

Shiny Red Apples
and Sugar Cookies

Winter Get-Together

After a vigorous skating session or hike in the snow, gather the group at your house for warming fare. This menu can be ready in minutes if the Souperburgers are prepared partially beforehand. Serve the soup in mugs. Arrange the other food on a buffet where guests can help themselves. Double or triple soups as needed.

Peanut Soup

¼ cup finely chopped celery
¼ cup finely chopped onion
2 tablespoons butter or margarine
1 can (10¾ ounces)
   condensed cream of
   chicken soup

⅓ cup peanut butter
1 soup can milk
Chopped peanuts

In saucepan, cook celery and onion in butter until tender. Blend in soup and peanut butter until smooth. Add milk. Heat; stir occasionally. Garnish with peanuts. Makes about 3½ cups.

Oyster Chowder

1 can (10½ ounces) condensed
   oyster stew
1 soup can milk
1 cup cubed cooked potatoes

½ cup diced cooked ham
1 tablespoon chopped parsley
⅛ teaspoon thyme, crushed

In saucepan, combine all ingredients. Heat; stir occasionally. Makes about 3½ cups.

❋ *Souperburger*

1 pound ground beef
½ cup chopped onion
1 tablespoon shortening
1 can (10¾ ounces) condensed
   chicken gumbo, golden
   mushroom, tomato,
   vegetable, or cream of
   mushroom soup

1 tablespoon prepared mustard
Dash pepper
Buns, split and toasted

In skillet, brown beef and cook onion in shortening until tender; stir to separate meat. Pour off fat. Add soup and seasonings. Cook 5 minutes; stir occasionally. Serve on buns. Makes about 3 cups.

Impromptu Supper

When you invite neighbors on the spur of the moment for a celebration or a gathering for newcomers, it helps to have some pantry-shelf specials to bring out. The menu should be easy to prepare but delectable. This one is. The dessert comes from the freezer — today's frozen layer cakes are a boon to the hurried hostess. Double or triple soups as needed.

❊ *Many Way Chowder*

¼ cup sliced celery
2 tablespoons chopped onion
1 tablespoon butter or margarine
1 can (10¾ ounces) condensed cream of mushroom or potato soup
½ soup can milk
½ soup can water

1 cup cubed cooked chicken or ham; or 1 can (about 7 ounces) minced clams or tuna, drained
½ cup cooked cut green beans, mixed vegetables, peas, or chopped canned tomatoes

In saucepan, cook celery and onion in butter until tender. Stir in soup; gradually blend in milk and water. Add remaining ingredients. Heat; stir occasionally. Makes about 4 cups.

Soup Mediterranean

1 can (2 ounces) sliced mushrooms, drained
Generous dash crushed oregano
1 tablespoon butter or margarine

1 can (10½ ounces) condensed minestrone soup
1 soup can water
½ cup cubed cooked beef, chicken, lamb, or pork

In saucepan, brown mushrooms with oregano in butter. Add remaining ingredients. Heat; stir occasionally. Makes about 3 cups.

❊ *Chili Soup*

1 pound ground beef
½ cup chopped green pepper
½ cup chopped onion
2 tablespoons chili powder
2 cans (11¼ ounces each) condensed chili beef soup

½ cup water
1 can (16 ounces) tomatoes, cut up
1 can (15½ ounces) kidney beans, undrained

In large saucepan, brown beef and cook green pepper and onion with chili powder until tender (use shortening if necessary). Stir to separate meat. Add remaining ingredients. Simmer 15 minutes; stir often. Makes about 8 cups.

Convenient Casserole Dinner

This is a dinner for casual entertaining. Guests will enjoy the Frisky Sours, a refreshing combination of beef broth and lemon juice. Bake the casserole in an attractive dish which can be brought to the table. Such a hearty casserole and big salad are a favorite menu for many a hostess and for guests. Make the cake "from-scratch" or start with a spice cake mix. This famous surprise cake (made with tomato soup as the liquid) has intrigued and pleased homemakers for more than 40 years.

Frisky Sours
Recipe may be doubled

1 can (10½ ounces) condensed
  beef broth
½ cup water

2 tablespoons lemon juice
6 ice cubes

Place all ingredients in a shaker; cover and shake well. Serve garnished with lemon twists. Makes about 1½ cups.

Cracked Ice: Omit water and ice cubes; substitute 1½ soup cans cracked ice.

Company Veal Casserole

2 pounds veal cutlet
  (about ½ inch thick)
Salt and pepper
½ cup chopped onion
2 large cloves garlic, minced
¼ cup butter or margarine
1 can (11 ounces) condensed
  Cheddar cheese soup
1 can (10¾ ounces) condensed
  cream of mushroom soup

⅔ cup milk
¼ cup Sauterne or other
  dry white wine
¼ cup chopped pimiento
3 cups cooked wide noodles
  (5 to 6 ounces uncooked)
2 packages (9 ounces each)
  Italian green beans,
  cooked and drained

Pound veal; sprinkle with salt and pepper. Cut into 1-inch pieces. In skillet, brown veal and cook onion with garlic in butter until tender. In 3-quart casserole, stir soups until smooth; gradually blend in milk, wine, and pimiento. Stir in veal mixture, noodles, and green beans. Bake at 350°F. for 40 minutes or until hot. 6 to 8 servings.

❋ *Tomato Spice Cake*

Pictured on back cover

2¼ cups cake flour or 2
   cups all-purpose flour
1⅓ cups sugar
4 teaspoons baking powder
1 teaspoon baking soda
1½ teaspoons allspice
1 teaspoon cinnamon

½ teaspoon ground cloves
1 can (10¾ ounces)
   condensed tomato soup
½ cup shortening
2 eggs
¼ cup water

Preheat oven to 350°F. Generously grease and flour 2 round layer pans, 8 or 9 inches, or an oblong pan, 13x9x2 inches. Measure dry ingredients into large bowl. Add soup and shortening. Beat at low to medium speed for 2 minutes (300 strokes with a spoon) scraping sides and bottom of bowl constantly. Add eggs and water. Beat 2 minutes more, scraping bowl frequently. Pour into pans. Bake 35 to 40 minutes. Let stand in pans 10 minutes; remove and cool on rack. Frost with *Cream Cheese Frosting*.

Bundt Pan: Proceed as above. Bake in well-greased and lightly floured 2½-quart bundt pan at 350°F. for 50 to 60 minutes or until done. Cool right side up in pan 15 minutes; remove from pan. Cool. If desired, sprinkle cake with confectioners' sugar.

❋ *Quick Tomato Spice Cake*

1 package (2 layer) spice cake mix
1 can (10¾ ounces) condensed
   tomato soup

½ cup water
2 eggs

Mix *only* above ingredients, following directions on package. If desired, fold in 1 cup chopped walnuts. Bake as directed. Frost with *Cream Cheese Frosting* or other favorite white frosting.

Cream Cheese Frosting

2 packages (3 ounces each)
   cream cheese, softened
1 package (1 pound) confectioners'
   sugar, sifted

½ teaspoon vanilla extract,
   optional

Blend cream cheese until smooth. Gradually blend in sugar and vanilla. If necessary, thin with milk. Makes enough frosting for two 8 or 9-inch layers.

TUREEN SUPPER

Tickets for the theater or a pops-concert call for a most special little supper — either before or after the fact. Famous hostesses have set a style for supper planned around a beautiful tureen of soup. Here's the chance to show off the heirloom soup container from Grandmother — with extra-special food. The tureen shown is a famous George III silver design of 1810 by Paul Storr who was a royal silversmith in England. Double or triple soups as needed.

Bisque a la Crab* or Chicken Soup New Orleans*

Romane, Avocado, and Grapefruit Salad

Hot Popovers

Raspberry Parfait

Nuts   Mints

Demitasse

❋ *Bisque A La Crab*

½ cup diagonally sliced celery
¼ teaspoon chervil, crushed
2 tablespoons butter or margarine
1 can (11 ounces) condensed Cheddar cheese soup
1 can (10¾ ounces) condensed cream of chicken soup

1½ soup cans milk
¼ cup sherry
2 packages (6 ounces each) frozen crab, thawed and drained (1½ cups)
⅓ cup sliced water chestnuts

In saucepan, cook celery with chervil in butter until tender. Stir in remaining ingredients. Heat; stir occasionally. Makes about 6 cups.

Lobster: Substitute 1½ cups cubed cooked lobster for crab.

Chicken Soup New Orleans

1 cup diced cooked ham
½ cup chopped onion
⅛ teaspoon thyme, crushed
Generous dash poultry seasoning
1 tablespoon butter or margarine
3 cans (10¾ ounces each) condensed chicken gumbo soup

3 soup cans water
1 cup cubed cooked chicken
1 package (10 ounces) frozen asparagus cuts, cooked and drained

In large pan, lightly brown ham and cook onion with thyme and poultry seasoning in butter until tender. Add remaining ingredients. Heat; stir occasionally. Makes about 10 cups.

**Soup-On-The-Rocks* or
Garden Asparagus Soup***

**Cornish Hens with
Orange-Honey Sauce***
**or Shrimp Kabobs with
Curry Sauce*** *(see index)*

Broccoli with Dill Butter
Cold Rice Vegetable Salad
Warm Poppy-seed Rolls
**Fruit Shortcakes
with Ice Cream**
Iced Coffee

Weekend Patio Party

This relaxing menu features one dish to be cooked on a rotisserie or grill out-of-doors. For the salad combine cold cooked rice, diced onion, sliced stuffed olives and celery with a tangy salad dressing. Chill. Make the biscuit shortcakes beforehand and serve two or three fruits such as strawberries, raspberries, and honeydew melon cubes for guests to make their own desserts. Cover the table with a pastel paper or cotton cloth and use pretty candles in hurricane lamps.

❋ *Soup-On-The-Rocks*

The easiest and most popular of frosted soups is yours to enjoy anywhere. Simply fill a broad glass with ice cubes. Pour beef broth, right from the can, over the cubes. Garnish with a slice or wedge of lemon or lime.

Note: For variety add a fleck of spice to the beef broth before pouring over ice cubes, perhaps curry, nutmeg, cinnamon, allspice, or ginger.

❋ *Garden Asparagus Soup*
Recipe may be doubled

1 can (10¾ ounces) condensed cream of asparagus soup	*½ soup can water*
½ cup sour cream	*½ teaspoon dried dill weed, crushed*
	Chopped cucumber or watercress

In saucepan, blend soup and sour cream; add water and dill. Heat; stir occasionally. Garnish with cucumber. Makes about 2½ cups.

Chilled Version: Increase water to 1 cup. Combine all ingredients; chill.

Cornish Hens with Orange-Honey Sauce

2 cans (10¾ ounces each) condensed chicken broth	*⅓ cup honey*
⅔ cup orange sections cut-up	*¼ cup cornstarch*
½ cup orange juice	*2 tablespoons lemon juice*
	½ teaspoon grated orange rind

In saucepan, combine all ingredients. Cook over low heat, stirring until thickened. Makes 3½ cups sauce.

Rock Cornish Hens *(Outdoor Method):* Truss 4 Rock Cornish Hens (about 1½ pounds each). Mount and balance hens close together and tie on spit. Place on rotisserie over glowing coals. Place drip pan under hens. Cook 45 minutes. Meanwhile, prepare sauce. Cook 45 minutes more or until tender, brushing frequently with sauce. Heat remaining sauce; serve with hens. 4 to 6 servings.

Rock Cornish Hens *(Indoor Method):* Roast 4 Rock Cornish Hens (about 1½ pounds each) at 400°F. for 45 minutes. Meanwhile, prepare sauce. Bake hens 30 minutes more or until tender, brushing frequently with sauce. Heat remaining sauce; serve with hens. 4 to 6 servings.

Provencal Picnic For Couples

Prepare a picnic for an outdoor get-together which features delectable dishes of Provence, that beautiful and romantic Mediterranean region of France. Robust and hearty, well flavored with garlic and herbs, the native fare is colorful and appealing. The soup will need to go in a big wide-mouth thermos or jug to keep hot.

Puree Mongole*
or
Beef Soup Riviera*
Salad Nicoise*
Buttered French Bread
Bel Paese Cheese
and Fresh Pears

✳ *Puree Mongole*

1 can (11¼ ounces) condensed
   green pea soup
1 can (10¾ ounces) condensed
   tomato soup

1 cup milk
1 cup water
Dash curry powder, optional

In saucepan, stir green pea soup until smooth; gradually blend in remaining ingredients. Heat; stir occasionally. Do not boil. Makes about 4½ cups.

Beef Soup Riviera
Recipe may be doubled

¼ cup sliced green onion
2 tablespoons butter or margarine
1 can (11 ounces) condensed
   beef soup

1 cup water
¼ cup orange juice
2 tablespoons toasted slivered
   almonds
2 orange slices, quartered

In saucepan, cook onion in butter until tender. Add soup, water, orange juice, and almonds. Heat; stir occasionally. Garnish with orange. Makes about 2½ cups.

Salad Nicoise

Dressing:

1 can (10¾ ounces) condensed
   tomato soup
½ cup salad oil
¼ cup wine vinegar
2 tablespoons sugar
1 tablespoon finely chopped onion
2 teaspoons dry mustard
1 teaspoon salt
¼ teaspoon pepper

Salad Ingredients:

4 cups sliced cooked potatoes
1 package (9 ounces) frozen cut
   green beans, cooked
   and drained
Salad greens
1 can (about 7 ounces) tuna,
   drained and flaked
1 medium tomato, cut in wedges
2 hard-cooked eggs, quartered
Ripe olives
Anchovy fillets

Combine soup, oil, vinegar, sugar, onion, mustard, salt, and pepper in a tightly covered container. Shake well. Mix potatoes with ¾ cup dressing and green beans with ¼ cup dressing. Chill all ingredients. On a large platter place salad greens. Arrange potatoes, green beans, and tuna; garnish with remaining ingredients. Serve with additional dressing. 4 servings.

TEENAGERS' DANCING PARTY

Teenagers will line up in a hurry to partake of this buffet with an Italian theme. For the fresh fruit kabobs, arrange alternately pineapple cubes, berries, red grapes, cubes of apple or peaches on small skewers and chill.

❋ *Meat-za Pizza*

*1 can (10¾ ounces) condensed tomato or Cheddar cheese soup**	*1 egg, slightly beaten*
1½ pounds ground beef	*1 teaspoon salt*
½ cup fine dry bread crumbs	*1 medium clove garlic, minced*
¼ cup finely chopped onion	*⅛ teaspoon oregano, crushed*
	3 ounces Mozzarella or mild process cheese, sliced

Mix thoroughly ½ cup soup with all ingredients except cheese; pat meat evenly on baking sheet into 10-inch circle with 1-inch stand-up rim. Or use a cookie sheet placing a 16-inch long sheet of aluminum foil (double thickness or heavy duty) on it, turning up edges and sealing corners to hold drippings. Bake at 450°F. for 10 minutes. Spoon off fat. Spread rest of soup on meat; top with cheese. Sprinkle with additional oregano. Top with mushrooms, anchovies, olives, or sausage, if desired. Bake 10 minutes more. Cut into wedges and serve. 6 servings.

*If using Cheddar cheese soup, substitute 4 slices tomato, cut in quarters for sliced cheese.

❋ *Coney Islands*
Recipe may be doubled

4 frankfurters, split lengthwise	*⅓ cup water*
1 tablespoon butter or margarine	*4 frankfurter rolls, split and toasted*
1 can (11¼ ounces) condensed chili beef soup	*Chopped onion*

In skillet, brown frankfurters in butter. Add soup and water. Heat; stir occasionally. Place frankfurters in rolls; spoon chili over. Top with onions. Garnish with shredded mild process cheese, sliced stuffed olives, chopped green pepper, or sliced pickles. Makes 4 sandwiches.

Meat-za Pizza and Coney Islands will attract all Teenagers who love to gather for hearty food after the big dance.

INDEX